A Book of
Short Stories
and
Memoirs

L. M. Starr

ISBN 979-8-88685-276-9 (paperback)
ISBN 979-8-88685-277-6 (digital)

Christian Faith Publishing
832 Park Avenue
Meadville, PA 16335
www.christianfaithpublishing.com

Printed in the United States of America

My name is L.M. Starr, and this book is filled with short stories and memoirs I have written in the '90s. I shall leave it up to you to decipher which is which. ("The truth does lie in the words.")

I will start my book with a story called "Willow Pond," dated November 1, 1997.

Willow Pond

November 1, 1997

WHERE TO BEGIN—WAS IT yesterday, a month ago, or longer? I'm not really sure. It's such a blur to me, and the thing is, well, no one would believe me if I told them anyway, at least I don't think anyone would.

It was a Saturday night, and the sky was clear and filled with beautiful stars that gave the road an endless look. I was driving home from work and inhaled the beauty of nature as I flew down interstate 59 with my windows open. Since I enjoyed nights like this, I decided to take a drive to my favorite spot, Willow Pond. It was located off the interstate around fifteen miles from my house.

The gravel road off the highway that led to the pond was kind of rough, and the trees on both sides of the road were very close together, which made the road look very narrow and long. I felt it was nothing for my Jeep and its four-wheel drive. The August air felt great blowing through the open windows. When I turned on the road to the pond, there were some roots that protruded through the gravel, and for some reason, the path to the pond was rougher than

I had remembered. I thought maybe the recent rain caused the roots to stick out more.

As I traveled along on this bumpy road, I think to myself, *Did I turn down the wrong road?* and suddenly, a big dip in the road, and **bam!** "Ouch!" I said as I hit my head.

It was a little after ten in the evening when I arrived at Willow Pond, and the sound of crickets filled the air. I parked my jeep in the pasture around twenty feet from the pond. After turning off the truck, I grabbed a beer from the cooler I had sitting next to me, put it in a huggy, then grabbed the lawn chair from behind the seat, and proceeded to the lake. It was time to sit on the lawn chair and enjoy the evening for a little while before going home to sleep.

There I was looking at the water while listening to the crickets harmonize around me. The stars in the sky radiated above me and gave the surroundings a peaceful glow. I breathed it in and gave out a big exhale! *This is the life*, I thought.

I opened my eyes and looked up and down then all around. A smile slowly surfaced on my face, and I felt as if I was one with nature. I was sitting there, savoring my bear when suddenly I heard an unusual sound. I looked up at the sky and saw an object whose size covered the circumference of the pond. The pond itself was oblong in shape and took up the space of four city blocks. My mouth dropped open for a moment, and then I shut it to force down a swallow of surprise. My eyes were asphyxiated on the object above the pond while my body sat frozen in the chair. I set the beer down, rubbed my eyes, and shook my head back and forth to make sure I wasn't dreaming. The object just sat there and hovered over the pond. My heart was beating faster as I slowly got up from the chair.

I took another forceful swallow and stepped forward to get a closer look at the object. As I was walking closer to the pond, a light illuminated from the center of the object above the pond. I felt as if my eyes were going to pop out of the sockets when an image appeared just above the pond. I forced a nervous smile that only showed on half of my face and took a step back. This image appeared on the water and started to walk toward me. My feet were frozen to the ground, and my head shifted back as it came closer and closer to me. "Move, feet, move!" I told myself. I stood there frozen in a state of bewilderment.

The figure kept getting closer and closer to me, and I could feel my heartbeat increase quicker and quicker as the image continued to get closer until it was standing in front of me.

I just stood there frozen, looking at it while it was looking at me. This figure looked like a human, but it didn't. It was a gray-ish-white misty-looking thing. Almost invisible-like in the sense that it could walk through anything—or me for all that matter. It was as if it took the mist off the pond to create its image. There were no fine features like legs or arms. It was basically the outline of a human, but not. I could almost see the trees behind this image.

Well, there I was, unable to move any part of my body with this image standing before me. Finally, my head tilted slightly to the left, and I found myself questioning what this thing wanted, and as I was doing this, the image lifted the upper left part of its body and reached toward my right arm. It gently touched my arm and pulled me toward it. I wanted to resist, but found myself moving in the direction of the pull. My heartbeat became normal, and I felt this overwhelming peace entering my body as I moved closer to this image. Our energies moved to the center of the beam, and suddenly, I was inside the object or energy force and questioned to myself what I was doing here.

The image that brought me to this place disappeared and left me in this space that was so white, I could barely keep my eyes open. After a few minutes, the brightness became so overwhelming I had to close my eyes and just stand there.

Great, I thought. *Now how am I going to be able to see anything if I can't keep my eyes open?* As soon as I finished that thought, I felt something lift me off the ground and take me up higher.

Oh, the elevation felt great, and the peace I felt inside became even stronger than before. I found myself asking questions out loud.

"Where am I?" "Am I dead?" "Who are you?" "Where are you?" and "Why can't I see you?"

Suddenly I stopped elevation, and my questions were answered one at a time, and though I was still blinded by the brightness around me, I felt the answers enter my mind from a force stronger than anything I had ever known.

"You are at the next level in life, which is beyond death, for death is a part of life which is a characteristic of the human condition.

"Yes, you have died, but it is not time for you to be here.

"I am a part of the spirit world you shall come to in time, and I am all around you and shall be when you return to the land of humans. You cannot see because of the purity that surrounds you. In time you shall attain this purity, but for now, it is time for you to go back to earth. There are many things for you to do there."

As I lay there in the position I was put in, more questions entered my mind. "I died. How did I die? Wasn't I just sitting at the pond drinking a beer, and what is it exactly that I'm supposed to do?"

"Yes, you died, and it happened when you were driving on the road to willow pond. After you hit the branch in the road, you were thrown from the truck, and the truck hit a tree just beyond the root. You hit your head on a rock fifteen feet from the area the truck hit. The reason you were sitting at the pond drinking a beer is because you were in between phases, and it was the most natural way for you to wait."

There I was, elevated in the spirit world that was so very peaceful, wondering why I had to go back. Then another question entered my brain.

"Willow pond is rarely visited. How is anyone going to know I'm out here?"

"Shortly after your truck hit the tree, it exploded. The flames were large enough to alarm the people that surrounded the area. In another moment. the medic will revive you. Before you are revived, you shall know all you are to do, but you will not remember it when you wake up. As you go through life, the doors you are to take shall be there for you to open. Some of the experiences will be better than others. But you must go through the doors to educate yourself as well as those around you. The world is walking on the path of uncertainty and is in need of guidance. The innocence you have shall help others to see more clearly. Some things you won't want to do but will be impelled to do. And know that you have been given the force needed to help you get through them. Always remember to believe in yourself with the actions you take in life. It shall take a couple of years before the first door will open because you must heal from the injury that has happened to you. Your memory has been stunned, but through time, you shall regain most of your past memories, and your sensitivity level shall increase. This will help you understand things in a different way than others. Your understanding shall help others."

Suddenly, I woke up and looked at the surroundings around me. I was in my room at my mother's house with an IV attached to my arm. I looked out the window to see it was dusk outside, and I was definitely not where I thought I was. (*Where was that?*) I took my hand and ran it through my hair—my hair! *What* happened to my *HAIR*!

I stood up quickly and fell back down because of the blood that just ran to my head.

"Oh, maybe I should not do that too quickly," I said.

I checked my pulse and realized I needed to take my time when I got up. I lay back down for a moment and looked around before I slowly got up. My head was throbbing in cadence with my heartbeat.

My mother was in the kitchen ten feet away from me, making what must have been supper. I looked up at the clock. "5:30 p.m." It was supper.

"Mom," I said with a weak voice.

She did not hear me, so I took a step closer and said it again. "Mom?"

"Yes, dear," she said, before realizing it was me talking to her.

"Sweetheart, you're awake!" She walked closer to me and gently held my arm and waist.

"Sit down, honey, I don't think you're supposed to be moving around. You finally woke up."

She said this as tears fell from her face and walked me to the sofa.

"Now you sit right here, and I am going to call the doctor to let him know you're awake. Oh, I was so worried about you. How do you feel? Let me call the doctor first and then we'll talk." She walked into the kitchen and continued talking to herself.

"She woke up. She woke up!"

Mom was crying all the way to the telephone and continued crying as she dialed the number. Dad came out of the bathroom and took the phone from Mom and asked for my doctor. Mom came back to sit by me. She just looked at me with tears falling from her face. We sat there and looked at each other, her with tears falling from her eyes and me just regaining some sort of consciousness. I could see from the circles under her eyes that she had not been getting much sleep. I just looked at her sad but happy face for a moment.

"I'm sorry, Mom, I didn't mean to worry you. Are you okay?"

"Yes, dear, you just put us through a terrible scare. We didn't know if you were ever going to come out of it or not."

My heart felt heavy as I looked at my mother, and with the weakness, I felt in my body I wrapped my arms around her and held her for a moment. I could feel the weight of the burden she was caring and tried to let her release her anguish on my shoulder. After Dad got off the phone, he came into the living room, and with a tear in his eyes, told me he was glad I was back. I tried to get up, but he gestured for me to stay and came to sit down on the other side of me. Then he gently held me in his arms and told me everything was going to be okay. The three of us just sat there for a moment, Mom holding one hand and Dad the other. I had never felt so much love before in my life. Tears began to trickle down my face.

"Mom, how long have I been unconscious?"

"Seven weeks, honey."

"How long was I in the hospital before you brought me home?"

"After three weeks, your father and I decided you could get the same care here with your sister. Since she is a practicing nurse, we felt it would be better for you to be in an environment you're used to."

"Karen is cool with the idea?"

"Of course, she is—which reminds me, we should give her a call to let her know you're awake."

Before Mom could get up, Dad gestured for her to stay with me while he went to the phone to call her. Mom turned to look at me, smiled, and gave me another hug.

"I'm so glad you're back with us."

"Me too," I said (though I'm not sure if I really meant it).

I looked up, and Dad was already off the phone.

"Your sister is on her way over here to see how you're doing."

He came to sit back down, and the three of us sat there until my sister arrived.

Fifteen minutes later, Karen was in the room, checking all my vitals.

"You could at least say hello before you start doing that."

"Sorry, sis, it's habit, I guess. How are you feeling?"

"A little weak, I guess, but other than that okay."

After she did all the checking she needed to do, she gave me a hug and sat on the floor in front of me. There we were, the four of us, the three of them staring at me, and I was just sitting there in kind of a daze. This went on for a few minutes until I finally said something to break the silence.

"Did I die?"

Karen looked at Mom and Dad, then me.

"Yes, you did die, and you were dead for about seven minutes before the medics on call that evening revived you. Is there anything you want to talk about?"

"Well, I just wanted to verify something."

"Verify something?" Karen said with a questionable look on her face.

"Yes, I had an experience when I died and wanted to make sure it wasn't just my imagination."

"Your imagination? What happened?" my mother asked.

I looked down to the floor and thought for a moment about what happened to me.

"I...ummm...died," I said as I looked at my sister. "Right?"

Karen reached over and put her hand on my right knee.

"Yes, you did, but you're going to be okay, sis. Don't worry."

"I'm not really worried about that. I mean something happened to me at Willow Pond. Something kind of weird. I mean I was shown what the rest of my life would entail, but I can't seem to remember any of that. At least not the specifics. Anyways, let me tell you what I remember...."

Thom Field

It was during the winter of 1975; the snow was coming down pretty hard on that Saturday evening when I went to Thom Field. After dinner, I put on my snow gear and went to have a fun-filled adventure with the snow. I had to walk four city blocks to get there, and it was all uphill. Once there, gerbil greeted me with a smile just before he glided down the hill. And gerbil was spelt with a little g. He was a friend of my brother, Matt. gerbil wasn't his real name, but it's the only one I knew him by. I never took the time to find out how he got such a name and didn't really care to. All I knew at that moment was the excitement of being one of the first people to go sledding in the fresh snow.

The hill itself wasn't that big because of the area it was located. There was a football field on the left side and its length reached all the way to Steuben Street, which was one long block away. The pool was on the right, and it faced the L-shaped road at the bottom. Twelfth Street was also next to the football field and was a dead end by the hill. The sledding area was right smack dab in the middle of the two and at the bottom was the road, which made it even more exciting to go sledding at Thom Field. The hill was just big enough to make it a challenge to get across the street and into the parking lot across from the pool, which only happened occasionally, so I decided not to take the challenge. Instead, I made a little snow jump near the bottom of the hill. I wanted to see how high and far I could go when I took it. I would occasionally stick my tongue out to catch the snowflakes as they fell from the sky. Oh, how I loved the snow, especially on walks when my footprints were the first to be made. Those white snowflakes would really sparkle once light hit them.

gerbil only stayed a little while.

"I'm going home, Lesley, see you later." He took his sled and went down the hill.

"See you, gerbil, I'm going to stay a little longer." I stayed about a half hour and decided to leave because my feet were numb, and it was getting late. I took the shortcut through the woods right above the hill. I started to walk up the path in the wooded area when suddenly I heard something. I stopped for a moment to listen. The noise was coming from a landing on the right made of rocks that could be climbed up to as well as down from. The rocks themselves protruded from the hill, and there was a flat area where people could sit and watch football games. I know because I watched a couple of games in the previous fall.

It wasn't fall at this particular time, and it was too cold to just sit and watch children go sledding. I began to walk a little closer, and as I did, I heard something that sounded like someone was struggling. My curiosity was getting the best of me, while at the same time I felt very nervous, so I quietly lay my body on the snow and inched my way closer to the noise. As I got closer, the noise became louder until finally, I was at the edge of the rock formation behind some thick brush. Thank goodness it was thick! Just five, maybe ten feet in front of me were two people struggling with each other. It sounded like women, though I really couldn't tell because of the snow gear each of them had on.

One of the women had the other in a headlock and was talking about a man she was in love with. She was apparently upset with the woman she had in a headlock, and though I couldn't see the two woman's faces, I knew something wasn't cool about the situation. The angry one was short and just barely fit in the blue snowsuit— which probably made her look a little heavier—while the other one looked a little taller and thinner. The short one was accusing the thin one of wanting too much. The thinner one was trying to get away but was unable to do so because of the tight grip around her neck.

Suddenly, I heard the sound of bones cracking, and the thin one went limp. The stocky one became nervous and tossed the thin one off the rocks onto a tree five feet below. The tree itself looked like lightning had struck it, striking off the top and leaving a jagged arrowhead point behind. The thin one landed on the jagged point back first, and it went right through her chest. The stocky one looked around, turned, and ran past me and out of the woods onto the road about thirty feet away.

I just lay there, frozen for a moment, grateful she did not see me wondering what I should do. I knew the woman who was pushed off the rocks was probably dead, and I had no idea who the other person was. Since I didn't know who it was, I decided to go someplace safe: home.

It took me five minutes to get home, and when I walked into the door, Mom was doing the dishes while Dad was watching TV. After I took off my snow gear, I sat down and looked at Mom, who was just finishing up the dishes.

"Mom, I just saw a murder."

"That's nice, dear."

"Mother, did you hear me? I just saw a murder at Thom Field!" When she realized what I said, she put down the towel and looked at me with a very surprised and worried look.

"John? Would you come in here please?" She walked away from the sink and sat down next to me at the kitchen table. "JOHN!"

"Yes, dear."

"Would you come in here please!"

"I'm coming, I'm coming." Dad got out of his chair in the living room, walked through the double doors into the kitchen, and sat down next to Mom. As soon as he sat down, I began to talk.

"I witnessed a murder at Thom Field," I said this while I rubbed my hands up and down my thighs to get both my fingers and legs warm. After I explained what I saw to my parents, my dad called the police while Mom held me in her arms. The police were at my house within ten minutes, and we immediately went to Thom Field. I was a little nervous when we drove there because of what I just saw there earlier. Within forty-five minutes, I was back at Tom Field. When we arrived, I was surprised to see another squad car already there. Immediately, Dad and the officer got out of the car and started to walk toward the rocks while Mom and I waited. I can still remember sitting in the squad car. We were unable to get out of the police car because we were in the back seat, locked in, and unable to open the door.

"Honey, I'm so sorry you had to see such a terrible thing. Are you sure you're okay?" my mother asked.

I nodded my head yes even though I knew I didn't mean it. I turned my face from hers and looked out the window of the squad car. I was going to forget that evening and pretend it never happened. This was exactly what I wanted to do: forget the whole thing. All I needed was a good night's sleep, and everything would be fine.

There we were, in the squad car, waiting, and while we were waiting, my mind kept going through the incident. I felt sick to my stomach and wanted to go home where it was safe.

Mom was holding me in her arms so tight, it was almost difficult to breathe. Within five minutes, my dad and the two officers came back with ghastly looks on their faces. One of the officers called an ambulance and a detective while the other came and talked to me. After he got into the squad car, he turned his head back and looked at me for a moment and then at my mother. "What happened?" he asked, and my mother turned her face toward mine.

"I watched two women fight with each other. The short one snapped the neck of the other and threw her off the rocks onto a tree," I said with an unsettling voice.

"You have to wait until the detective comes before you can leave."

Great! I thought as I rested my head on my mom's shoulder and closed my eyes. Mom's tight grip loosened as she stroked my hair with her right hand. She then looked at the officer, then me, and then back at him again before she opened her mouth.

"Don't you think my daughter has explained enough for now? It is getting late, and she is tired. Can't this wait until morning?" As she finished this statement, Detective Armstrong showed up at her window. I had to tell the story one more time before my parents and I were taken home.

Once we were dropped off at home, I put my pajamas on, walked through the kitchen, and into the living room where the stairs to go upstairs were. Mom was sitting on the Lazy Boy next to the window on the right, and Dad lounged on the sofa next to the stairs to go upstairs. I walked up to Dad and gave him a big hug. He reciprocated.

"Lesley, if you need to talk about what happened tonight—"

"I'm okay, Dad."

"Are you sure?"

"Yes, Daddy, I'm okay—really, I am. I'm just tired from the event. I want to try and get some sleep. I'm just tired."

"Okay, honey, love you. Good night."

"Love you too, Dad."

I went over to my mom and gave her a big hug.

"Good night, Mom."

"Good night, Lesley. Try to get some sleep."

I nodded okay and went to go upstairs. As I walked up the stairs, my mind kept thinking about what happened that night. I said I was tired, but as I took each step on those stairs, I questioned whether or not I could sleep.

My question was answered within the first hour. I just kept tossing and turning; the image of that woman's body continuously taunted me throughout the night. I could picture her with the jagged edge trunk shoved through her chest. Pieces of intestines and blood were mixed in with the vinyl of the snowsuit. Her body was limp and bent backward from the impact of falling. Her hands twitched for a long moment while her eyes screamed in despair.

"Help me!" From where she lay was a perfect view of me. She looked right at me. I just looked at her while a feeling of hopelessness shot through my body. Our eyes were locked for what felt like an eternity until hers went blank and her body went even limper. Man, it was gross. She didn't want to die. I could tell by her expression. Yet there she was, dead! I wondered how old she was. What if the other person saw me? No, at least I wouldn't let myself believe it. That night, I only slept for about three hours.

The next morning, two parents greeted me with peppy smiles.

"Good morning, Lesley."

"Good morning."

"How are you feeling this morning, Lesley?" my mother asked.

"Fine." I said this even though I felt exhausted from lack of sleep.

"Everything will be fine, Lesley."

"I know, Mom." I made an attempt to smile, but found a heavy sigh came out of my mouth much quicker. My mother put a plate of eggs, hash browns, and a biscuit on the kitchen table for me to eat. I grabbed the ketchup from the refrigerator and sat down. It seemed as soon as I put the ketchup on the hash browns, my appetite went out the window. Visions of the tree with fragments of her intestines suddenly dashed through my brain and almost made me vomit. Shortly after breakfast, the police called and told my dad I needed to go to the police station to make a statement. After Dad hung up the phone, he turned to ask Mom if she wanted to go. But before he could finish the sentence, she handed him his jacket and put on her own.

It took five minutes to get to the police station, and I was trying to stay calm even though I didn't want to go there.

"John, I want us both to be with her through the questioning."

"Yes, Maggs. Now, Lesley, if at any time you want to stop talking, let us know," my dad said softly.

"Okay, Dad," was my reply as I looked out the window.

When we went into the building, one of the officers greeted us as we walked in. He appeared to know we were on our way, for he gestured for us to follow him, and he took us into a small room with a rectangle table and four chairs and asked us to wait while he got Detective Armstrong. We sat there and waited for what felt like an eternity. Dad was sitting with his hands crossed while Mom had a difficult time sitting still. After ten minutes passed, Detective

Armstrong opened the door and entered the room with a somber look on his face.

He stood about six feet tall and looked very thin in his navy-blue suit. He was about my parent's age and had the most striking blue eyes I had ever seen. His face had strong features, which allowed him the luxury of intimidation. Yet his aura was very gentle. He sat down next to me and looked at my thirteen-year-old face.

"How are you doing?"

"Fine," I said, even though I didn't mean it.

He was very attentive to my age when he asked me questions, and the first one he asked was a stupid one.

"Why were you at Thom Field?" I looked at my mother and then back at him.

"To go sledding."

He could tell by the look on my face that I thought it was a stupid question and smiled.

"Lesley, I know you have told the story a few times already, but I need you to tell it again." I put my right elbow on the table and rubbed my upper forehead with my fingers. I looked at the door behind him and started to talk.

"I was at Thom Field, sledding. When I thought it was time to go home, I took the shortcut through the wooded area behind the hill. There is a path that leads to the street on top of it. When I started to walk up the path, I heard something to my right. I stopped and listen for a moment and decided to walk toward the noise when I heard a muffled voice.

"'Stop your meddling, woman, you're starting to annoy me with your greedy pocket!' The tall woman said.

"I dropped down to the ground and started to crawl across the snow-covered path toward the noise. I inched my way up to some shrubs and stopped when I noticed two people wrestling on the rocks. I lay there frozen as I watched them and tried to be as quiet as I could."

"Do you think you were noticed?" Detective Armstrong asked in a stern voice.

"I don't think so."

"Are you sure?"

"Yes!" After telling the story a couple of times, the detective thanked me for the information and told my parents he would get back in touch with me if he needed to.

When I walked into the house, I grabbed the newspaper out of the mailbox. On the cover was a picture of Unga Farrett. The heading above her picture was *"The mysterious death of Unga Farrett."*

It also mentioned the name of her husband, Albert Farrett, who apparently sold real estate and was very rich. (For the first time in my life, I read the newspaper.)

This guy Albert was married before to a woman who had a health condition. What kind of condition *it* was, the paper didn't say. After I read the paper, I didn't know what to think, and within twenty minutes, I decided not to think about it at all.

Talk about what happened began to circulate throughout the city of Wausau. And though my name was not mentioned in any of the papers, I felt exposed. Detective Armstrong told me everything would be okay. Yet I couldn't help but feel different. I suddenly felt older.

The next couple of days were filled with sleepless nights and restless days, the memory of what I saw continued to haunt me. My appetite decreased as my nightmares increased. After one week, my parents became worried and took me to a doctor.

Again we waited for ten minutes before I was seen, and yes, it felt like an eternity. Only I went in to talk to the doctor. His name: Anthony Squid; his title: psychiatrist.

As I walked into his office, I could not believe the size of it, or the type of decorative devices he had on the walls either. On the left, the entire wall was a sand picture. It was mounted into the wall whose depth was around nine inches, and the sand picture was centered in the wall. This way it could move back and forth a little. It just sat there with a sunset-type look about it. Its design was odd, for when I moved from one place to another, it changed. His desk was in front of a totally windowed wall with a view of downtown Wausau. On the right wall, he had a giant picture of a maze, and in the center, it said: "To the center of peace." It was a square-type maze with several openings a person could start from, and it was set into the wall about twelve inches. It had little square boxes at certain dead-end points, and each one had a lock on it.

Odd, I thought.

He gestured for me to sit down.

"Thank you," I said.

"My name is Dr. Squid, Dr. Anthony Squid. I understand you are not eating or sleeping well, Lesley. Would you like to talk about anything?" he said with softness in his voice. I looked at him, and though his voice was soft, I felt uncomfortable and wanted someone there with me.

"Dr. Squid, I would like my mother to be here with me right now, okay?"

"I'll go get her." He stood up and walked to the door while I sat there, looking at the maze. "To the Center of Peace." I stood up, walked to the maze, and with my finger, made my first attempt. I was just getting started when Dr. Squid and my mother walked in.

"I see you're trying to figure out the maze, Lesley?"

"Sort of. What are the little boxes for?"

"It does give the puzzle a little puzzle to figure out now, doesn't it, Lesley?" He replied with an undertone in his voice.

"What?" was my response with a questionable look on my face.

He walked up the maze and pointed at the boxes. "The boxes indicate each trail made. The letter on each box is the first initial of those who made an attempt."

I counted the boxes in the maze.

"Looks like several have already tried." He walked away from the maze and toward the sand picture.

"Yes, but none have found it." He said this with a mysteriously odd chuckle afterward.

I turned from the maze to look at him. He was standing in front of the sand picture, and my mother stood next to him. I looked at her.

"Mom, I really don't think I need to be here."

"Honey, your father and I are worried about you. You haven't been eating or sleeping well lately, and we are concerned."

"Mom, I'm okay, I just keep seeing that woman with the branch shoved through her chest, and it kind of affects me."

"That's why we are here."

"Mother, I do not need to see a shrink to get better. I need to forget about what I witnessed at Thom Field."

"Lesley."

"It's okay, Lesley, you don't have to talk to me. Why don't you go by your dad and let me talk to your mother?"

"Thank you, I will!" I left my mother with him and sat with my dad for over ten minutes. When she came out of the office, I stood up and looked at her. "What took you so long?"

"He just wanted to tell me to be patient with you, Lesley."

"Oh, can we go now?"

"Yes, we can go."

* * * * *

Within a couple of weeks, I was eating and sleeping better. The nightmares subsided, and life seemed to be normal again. I wished that horrible evening away and felt I successfully did it. Life was good again; at least this is what I thought until the phone rang. I was eating a popsicle when my mother answered it. Her usual happy voice changed shortly after she said hello.

I was still eating my popsicle at the kitchen table when Mom turned and looked at me.

"Lesley, that was Detective Armstrong, and he wants to talk to you again." My popsicle fell off the stick unto the table. My heart did the same, but into my stomach.

"Why?"

"He found some new evidence and feels you can help him understand it."

"New evidence—how could new evidence make my story any different?"

"Lesley, he said it was important. Now pick up your mess, wash your hands, and let's go."

"All right already. I don't know why he has to talk to me. I've told him everything." At this particular moment, as I washed my hands, a realization of things never being the same encompassed my body. I looked at myself in the mirror and wiped the tears from my eyes. What I considered a nightmare was a reality, and I could no longer hide from it. I grabbed my jacket and went into the car.

"I'm sure this won't take long. He probably just wants to reassure us about everything."

"Yeah, Mom, whatever."

As soon as Mom and I walked into the police station, every officer in the room became quiet, and Detective Armstrong walked with us to the questioning room. I sat down in one of the chairs, put my hand under my chin, and my pinky was resting on my lips.

"I'm sorry I had to call you back, but some new evidence has surfaced, and I'm a little concerned."

"Concerned about what?" I asked with a concerned look on my face.

"There is a rumor out there that someone witnessed the murder. And though it's not known who this someone is, it won't be long before it hits the news."

"How did a rumor start? I thought you were not going to tell anyone!"

"I didn't, Lesley, but somehow it leaked out. Lesley, were you seen?"

"*No*! I told you, there wasn't anyone out there but those two people and me. I was hidden by some brush."

"I know you told me, Lesley. Do you still think it was a woman?"

He said this with concern and impatience.

"I'm pretty sure, though they did have scarfs on which would change the voice a little. It might have been a man, a short man with a non-masculine voice."

The detective leaned against the table and smiled. "I'm just making sure of everything, Lesley."

"Now what?" My mother asked this question with directness in her voice.

"I've requested double security around the area you live in." My mother looked at him in a condescending manner.

"Is that supposed to make us feel better?" Mother grabbed my hand and pulled me closer to her.

"It will make it more difficult for anyone to find you."

I looked away from him and toward the door. Thirteen years old, and I had to face the possibility of death. Death by some crazy woman who doesn't want me alive. I looked at my mother, who suddenly just snapped.

"More difficult to find her—what do you mean? Does this person know Lesley was there? Do you need to be worrying my little girl like this?"

"No, I'm just making her aware of it, Maggs."

"So now what?"

"Now the two of you can go home, and we will be in touch."

"Thank you, Detective. Let's go, Lesley."

"Okay, Mom."

After the meeting, everything around me changed. No longer did I walk the streets in the carefree way I used to. I became more conscious of everything around me. It got to the point where I could hear a pin drop two rooms away.

A week had gone by, and I became a walking zombie. I was averaging two to three hours of sleep a night, and it showed.

"Lesley, I'm going to make you another appointment to see Dr. Squid."

"Mo-om, I don't want to go there."

"Lesley, you need to talk to someone, and he is a professional."

"I'll go, but I really don't think it matters."

Two days later, I went to see Dr. Squid.

* * * * *

Mom made the appointment for 10:00 a.m., and we were in his office by 9:57 a.m.

"Lesley, appointment at ten with Dr. Squid."

"Have a seat. I'll tell him you are here."

"Mom, how long will this take?"

"I'm not sure, honey. Be patient." As soon as my mother finished, the secretary came up to us.

"Lesley, Dr. Squid is ready to see you." I looked at her then at Mom.

"Okay." When I walked into his office, he was standing by the window looking out.

"Sit down, Lesley."

I decided to go and sit in his chair by the window. "Do you mind if I sit here?"

"If you like."

"I don't know exactly what my mom thinks you can do for me, but the only reason I am here is because of her."

"Do you want to talk about anything?"

"Like is there anything I am supposed to tell you?"

"Your mom seems to think so, and by the circles under your eyes, I would have to agree with her."

"My mother worries too much." I stared out the window, and there was a long moment of silence. "Things are different for me at school now."

"What do you mean?"

"Ever since that night."

"What are you talking about Lesley?" A heavy sigh came out of my mouth, followed by silence.

"The night I saw a woman murdered."

"What woman?"

"I'm sure my mother has told you."

"Told me what, Lesley?"

"Unga Farrett! Does the name ring a bell for you, Doctor?"

"Ah yes, the woman who was found at Thom Field." When he said this, his eyes looked out the window with a vacant look in them. He slowly turned to look at me with his best attempt to look empathetic. He stepped away from the window and walked closer to me.

"What do you know about her death?"

"Nothing. I think I would like my mother in here now."

He looked at me and then walked out of the office.

I dropped my head back and let out another weighty sigh of tension. I looked at his desk only to see a picture of him in his golf attire. A short guy who, in this portrait, wore a yellow sweater that made him look chunkier. He had these brown eyes, these very beautiful brown eyes that changed with his mood. Not that his eyes changed in the portrait; they just changed in front of me when he walked away from the window. I was clueless as to where my mother found him; though my parents' income might have had something to do with it.

I stood up and went to look at the maze. I looked at the openings and then at the boxes, those little square boxes. One had the letter k, another l, and yet another a. All of them lowercase letters. The center had a ring imprint C on it. Suddenly, I felt someone's breath on my neck.

"Dr. Squid, you startled me."

"Interesting maze. Would you like to try?"

"No, thank you." I looked at him and then at my mom.

"Mom, I am real tired of being here. Can he give me something to help me sleep?" I looked at the doctor.

"Can you, Doctor?"

"Yes, I can."

"Then can we have the prescription so I can go?"

"Could I talk to your mother alone for a moment, Lesley?"

"Sure, hurry, Mom."

"Okay, Lesley." It only took five minutes, and we were out the door.

"Thanks, Mom."

"We're going to pick up the prescription, and when we get home, I'm going to give you one, so you can get some rest."

As Mom pulled into the driveway, a police car pulled up in front of the house.

Mom reassured me, "I'm sure he is just here to make sure you're okay, honey."

I replied, "What on earth for?"

As we got out of the car, the policeman said "Detective Armstrong would like to talk to her again."

"She is not going. Tell Detective Armstrong he can come here, and not until my daughter takes a nap."

"He said it was urgent."

"Urgent! My daughter's rest is urgent. You call him and tell him she needs some rest. There is a phone in the house."

We all walked into the house together, and he made the phone call.

"Detective Armstrong will come here in the morning, ma'am. Sorry about the inconvenience."

"Have a nice day, officer." After she shut the door behind the officer, my mom gave me the pills to help me sleep, and I lay down and took a nap. I slept until nine o'clock the next morning. I woke up to breakfast I could eat: cereal and toast.

By ten o'clock, Detective Armstrong was sitting at the kitchen table, patiently waiting for me to get out of the bathroom.

"Good morning, Lesley. How are you feeling today?"

"Morning, Detective. You're here early. What's up?"

"We found Mr. Farrett's ex-patient. Sarah and I would like you to come down to the station and verify if it was her you saw that night."

"How am I supposed to do that? If you remember what I told you, she was in a snowsuit, and her face was covered."

"I know, but this is the only way we have to identify the killer."

Before the detective and I finished, Mom was already waiting with jackets.

"This woman will not be able to see my daughter, will she?"

"No, Lesley will be in a different room where she will be able to see and hear her. Will your husband be coming too?"

"No, he is out of town for business."

She then looked at me and then back at him.

"We'll follow you, Detective." Mom and I got into the car and drove to the police station.

"This won't take long, honey. All you have to do is identify this woman, and it will all be over."

I just sat there and listened while my heart was beating a nervous beat. I thought to myself, *could I identify a woman just by her voice?* I wasn't sure, but was I ever edgy.

When we walked into the police station, every eye was on me. It made me uncomfortable. Detective Armstrong took us to a room where we waited. We waited for about half an hour. I was sitting in that chair, looking through the window of fate. I knew a woman was going to enter the room on the other side, and I was going to forecast her destiny. I didn't like the feeling, yet I wanted to feel free from the nightmare that haunted me. Finally, the door opened, and Detective Armstrong and Sarah entered the room. She was short, but not as chunky as I remembered. Maybe the snowsuit made her look chunkier. My mind flashed back; it was snowing pretty hard that night, but the woman did look chumpy. The moment she opened her mouth, I knew it wasn't her. This woman's voice was softer.

"Mom, it's not her."

"Are you sure?"

"Yes, this woman is thinner and her voice is softer."

"Sweetie, you know the snowsuit would make her look bigger."

"I know, Mom, but her voice is too soft."

"Yes, but, Lesley, she is not talking in an angered tone."

As Mom was saying this, the detective was agitating Sarah to the point of an outburst.

"*I told you I had nothing to do with that woman's death!* I wasn't even in Wausau at the time it happened."

"It just doesn't sound like her, Mom." Mom let out a heavy sigh.

"It's okay, honey."

The detective and Sarah left the room, and within five minutes, he walked into the room Mom and I were in.

"Was it her?"

"No."

"Are you sure, Lesley?"

"I am more than sure! It wasn't her."

"She fits the description you gave us, Lesley, and she had a reason to kill Unga."

"Why?"

"Mr. Farrett stopped supporting her a month before the death."

"Oh, well, it's not the same voice, Detective Armstrong."

"We're going to hold her until the alibi checks out."

"Fine, can we go now?"

"Yes, you can go." Mom and I stood up and left. As we walked out of the police station, Sarah was sitting by a sergeant's desk. Our eyes locked as I walked out the door, and she smiled at me.

"That was a smart place for the detective to take her, Mom, wasn't it?"

"You said she didn't do it, Lesley."

"I know, Mom, but he did not know it until he came into the room with us."

"Mm, you have a point. Why would he do such a foolish thing?"

"And now she knows who I am."

"You said she didn't do it, Lesley."

"I know, but it bothers me that she knows who I am." Twenty minutes after we were home, Mom decided she needed to see Dr. Squid—not me; her. She didn't want me to be alone, so I went with her. It wasn't until after she said this that I realized there were dark circles under her eyes.

"Maybe he will give you some sleeping pills to help you sleep. It helped me."

"I know, honey, but since your dad is out of town and won't be back for a while, I don't think it would be wise to take sleeping pills."

"Maybe he can give you a smaller dosage—you know, to help you calm down so you can fall asleep."

"Maybe." A heavy sigh followed her word.

As we were walking down the corridor to his office, Sarah was just leaving with a piece of paper in her hand. She looked right at me as we passed each other. I watched her walk into the elevator.

"She came out of his office, Mother."

"I know. She could be one of his patients. The paper did say she had a health condition."

"Something doesn't seem right here, Mother."

"Lesley, he is a doctor, she is a patient. Please don't read anything more into it."

"She is also a murder suspect, mother."

When we walked into his office, he seemed a little surprised. After he gathered his composure, he greeted us with a smile.

"I wasn't expecting you so soon. What can I do for you?"

He looked at my mom when he said this, almost as if he didn't notice my presence at all. My eyes were not looking at him so pleasantly at the time, and I spoke before my mother could say a thing.

"How do you know Sarah?"

"She was a patient of mine when—"

"Was a patient?"

"Yes, Lesley."

"Is she your patient now?"

"She only wanted her pills prescribed for her."

"Is it legal for you to be seeing me, Doctor?"

"Why wouldn't it be?"

"Because you were her doctor?"

"Was, Lesley—past tense. She hasn't been my patient since the divorce. Now what is it I can do for you, Maggs?"

"First, I would like to know: if Sarah isn't your patient anymore, why was she seeing you today?"

"I can understand your concern, Maggs. First of all, I cannot tell you why she was here because it is confidential information between my patient and me. Secondly, she is not seeing me anymore because there was no need to. Apparently, the information about Unga has her a little stressed, and she wanted a prescription filled."

"I was wondering if you could prescribe me something a little weaker than you gave my daughter?"

"Sure I could, Maggs. Take it about half an hour before you go to bed."

"Thank you, Doctor." That was it—end of conversation. My mother and I left, knowing he knew Sarah. I told myself to relax yet found it difficult not to jump to any conclusions. After we filled her prescription, we went home, and to my surprise, Dad was there. He greeted me with a hug, and I could tell by Mom's eyes she was glad he was home.

"You're home early, John."

"After talking with you the other night, I decided I needed to be here with the two of you."

"Thanks, Dad."

I gave him a kiss on the cheek and went into the living room, so they could talk. When I looked back, they were hugging each other, and as he held her, a tear fell from her face. It was good that Dad came home; it made the house feel safer.

Shortly after we were home, Mom started to make supper. Since she used up all the milk for the potatoes, I needed to go buy more at the store. It was only a four-block walk, and it was all flat land. Three police cars drove past me before reaching the store. This gave me a strange sense of security. I quickly went to get the milk and stood in line. There were two checkouts open, and each had four people waiting. I chose the line with people who had the least amount of items. After a couple of people left, another person stood behind me.

"Hello, Lesley."

It was Sarah! I could feel my eyes widening and jaw gripping when I turned to look at her. Within a millisecond, I responded.

"Hello."

"I heard you watched Unga die." As she said this, the cashier ran the milk through the scanner.

"That will be ninety-seven cents please."

I gave the cashier a dollar bill.

"Paper or plastic?"

"Plastic." After she gave me the change, I left without saying another word to Sarah. As I was walking across the parking lot, I noticed a black BMW with Dr. Squid in it. The car was running, and he was looking at some paper. When I realized he didn't see me, I slid underneath some black tarp in the back of an old truck. There were several rusted-out areas in the back, which made it easy for me to look out. Dr. Squid's vehicle was on the opposite side of the lot, and I was able to see him clearly. Sarah finally came out of the store and was looking around as she walked toward his car. I watched as she opened the passenger door and climbed in. After she got in, they talked for a moment and then left. I waited until I could no longer see them and ran home. I ran in between houses, so I wouldn't be seen. I didn't notice any police cars on the way back which made me more nervous. By the time I entered the house, supper was ready.

"What took you so long?"

"The lines were long."

"Oh, it is kind of busy at this time, isn't it?"

The three of us sat down and ate dinner. I didn't mention what happened at the store because I felt it would worry Mom.

The next morning, I went to get the paper out of the mailbox, and on the front cover was another shocking story. The title of this one said: *"Ex-wife commits suicide."*

I dropped the paper on the floor. When I went to pick it back up, I bumped my head on the kitchen table.

"Ouch!"

"Be careful, Lesley."

My mother said this as she walked past me and into the bathroom. I looked at the table as I rubbed my head.

"Was the table always so close to the door?"

"Yes, it was. You just need to look where you're going." I immediately sat down. The paper stated she was found in the bathtub and had apparently fallen asleep and drowned. There was a bottle of sleeping pills on the floor along with a suicide note under the bottle giving the reason for her actions. It was a confession to the murder of Unga. I was taken aback by the news, yet relieved. Now I could sleep at night. Yet something didn't seem right. Sarah's voice wasn't the one I heard that night, and she left the store with Dr. Squid. Something felt very wrong. Thoughts went rampant in my mind. I was really becoming very suspicious about Dr. Squid and decided to go visit him.

* * * * *

When I walked into his office, I was surprised to see Detective Armstrong.

"What are you doing here?"

"I could ask you the same question, Lesley."

"She is a patient of mine, Detective, and it's time for her appointment. Is there anything else you need to know?"

"No, the case is almost closed. I just wanted to verify your relationship with Sarah."

"As I stated earlier, she was a patient of mine. She wanted an old prescription filled. Under the circumstances, I felt it appropriate. She could not have overdosed on the pills, for according to you, there were twenty-eight left. Which means she only took two. Though the empty bottle of wine probably contributed to the situation. She has told me more than once death by drowning was a good way to die."

"Thank you for your time, Doctor."

This was the end of their conversation, and Detective Armstrong left. There was a moment of silence as he walked to the window.

"So soon I see you, Lesley, and without your mother. How nice of you to do that."

"Where were you last night?"

"My, my, such an angered tone. Why do you ask?"

He turned away from the window and stepped closer to me. At that moment I was unsure of what to do next and decided to walk to the maze. As I did this, he picked something up from the desk and walked to the maze too.

"Ready to give it a try?"

I looked at him and then at the maze.

"Not really." He put an s on one of the little boxes. "I saw you with her last night."

"I know. Sarah told me when I took her home."

"Does that mean you have nothing to hide?"

"What would I have to hide? She asked for a ride home because her car was in the shop. That's it. I dropped her off and left. I didn't even go inside."

He looked at me, smiled, and walked to his desk. I looked at the little s put on one of the boxes.

"Sarah tried the maze?"

"Yesterday, before I took her home."

"She got pretty far."

"Actually, the farthest. I told her I would make sure to mark the spot."

"What does the 'C' stand for?"

"Courage."

"Courage?"

"Yes, it takes courage to go at something so big."

"Whatever. I don't think I will need to see you anymore, Doctor." When I said this, I walked toward the door to leave.

"Since it's over, there is no need to."

"Is that why you came here?"

"Yes."

I said this to avoid embarrassment.

"Thank you for doing that, Lesley."

"Goodbye, Dr. Squid."

"Goodbye, Lesley."

I left his office and was surprised to see Detective Armstrong waiting for me.

"Hello, Lesley."

"Hi, Detective, I thought you left."

"I wanted to talk to you."

"It's over, Detective."

"I know, Lesley. How are you feeling?"

"How am I feeling? I thought I just left the psychiatrist's office."

"Need a lift?"

"Sure."

We were walking to his car when I noticed gerbil go into the building.

"Odd," I said. "I wonder why he's going in there?"

"Who?"

"gerbil, the other person at Thom Field on the night of Unga's death."

"Really? Interesting. Many people see psychiatrists these days, Lesley. He probably had an appointment with one of the doctors."

"There are several of them in there too, aren't there?"

"As a matter of fact, Lesley, there are."

As he unlocked the door, I looked up at the doctor's window. gerbil was looking out the window, and his eyes were locked on mine. I looked at the detective, who gestured for me to get into the car and then back up at the window. He was gone.

"What's wrong, Lesley?"

"Nothing."

I shut the car door and put my seat belt on.

"I thought I saw something, that's all."

"By the look on your face, it wasn't pleasant."

"Pleasant—it's the thought that disturbs me."

I sat in his car and questioned what I saw.

"The case is pretty closed, right, Detective?"

"Yes, it is. We have the written confession. Now you can rest easy, Lesley."

"Things are different, Detective."

"In what way?"

"Come on, Detective Armstrong."

He stopped the car in front of my house. Just before I got out of the car, I looked at him and smiled.

"Do you think Sarah killed Unga?"

"That is what the suicide note said, Lesley."

"Bye, Detective Armstrong."

"Bye, Lesley."

While I was walking to the house, I heard his CB go on.

"Detective Armstrong, this is dispatch. The alibi for Sarah checks out."

"Thank you, dispatch, out."

I was at the front door when he looked up at me and smiled. I waved goodbye and went inside. Mom and Dad were both at the kitchen table with relieved expressions on their faces. Dad pointed at the paper and smiled.

"It's over, Lesley."

I smiled and sat down on the chair closest to the door.

"So it says, Dad."

"Maybe we could go out and eat. What do you think, Maggs?"

"It's okay with me. What do you think Lesley?"

"Could we stay here—you know, order out? Maybe Dad could put some logs in the fireplace."

"What do you think, John?"

"Sounds okay to me."

After everyone agreed, Dad went to the garage to get some wood while Mom ordered a pizza and garlic bread for lunch. I went into the living room and waited for Dad to get the fire going. I wanted to watch the flames shoot off its decorative designs. It was a great way to get my mind in a more relaxed state. As the flame flickered, I thought about the pleasant times in my life where everything made sense and murder only happened on TV. I let out a heavy sigh and allowed my body to become relaxed. The more I allowed myself to become mesmerized by the flames, the more my body relaxed. Thirty minutes later, the pizza arrived, and with it, my growling stomach. After lunch, I sipped on a cup of hot chocolate by the kitchen window. The clouds rolled in, and it started snowing. It was the perfect day to go sledding. I looked at the clock.

2:30 p.m. "Mm."

I looked away from the clock and back outside. The snow was falling even harder, making my visual perception weak. The hot chocolate felt nice in between my hands. I took a sip and looked back outside.

"Maybe later."

The End

Mile Marker 101

November 23, 1996

IT WAS A SATURDAY morning on November 23 in 1996 when I found myself in a somewhat uncomfortable situation on interstate 39N at mile marker 101. I was headed toward Wausau, Wisconsin.

The day started out early on that Saturday morning in Madison. The alarm clock went off at seven o'clock, and I got up to listen to the weather report. The weather channel said the roads were slippery, and the conditions would worsen throughout the day. I needed to be in Wausau for my niece's baptism on Sunday, and since I was asked and accepted to be the godmother of my niece Katrina, I felt it was important that I be there for her baptism. I decided to leave early before the roads worsened.

It was around eight o'clock in the morning when I left my apartment on West Washington Street, and since I needed gas, I stopped at a gas station on East Washington to fill up my tank. While I was there, I asked opinions on whether it was safe to travel to Wausau, and the overall consensus was to drive carefully. So after I filled the tank, I left the gas station and started to drive on East Washington toward Interstate 90/94. I drove slower than most of the traffic, for my car would slide quicker because the tires on my car were worn. When I entered Interstate 90/94, the traffic traveled at about fifty-five miles per hour.

Initially, the roads seemed okay. The fast lane was only used to pass because it was sloppier than the slow lane. It wasn't long before I was on Interstate 39N (Highway 51), and the speed of traffic was the same on 39 as it was on 90/94. Well, as I drove along, I noticed there was a slow driver who traveled very slowly. I needed to slow up because there were two cars that at that moment passed me on the left. So I gently pumped my brakes and slowed down behind the slow car in front of me.

When the two cars passed me, I put my blinker on and went behind them. Well, as I started to pass the slower driver, the car in front of me started to brake, and I began to feel a little uncomfortable. So as soon as that car moved to the slow lane, I passed on the left. Shortly after I passed the car on the right, my car hit a slippery spot and started to swerve.

As my heart skipped a beat, I tried to compensate for the swerve and turned the steering wheel in the same direction, but the car did not correct itself. Instead, the car just swerved a little harder to the right. I thought to myself: *Oh, shit! Now what am I supposed to do?* and decided that I had no control of the car and let it do as it wished while I tried to relax. What a moment that was. As the car started to spin, my heart beat a little faster, and for a moment I looked at traffic head-on, as in face to face!

A millisecond later, I was faced in the right direction, only I was on a field in about two inches of snow. I just sat there for a moment and released the clutch, which of course made the car choke and shut off. I got out of the car and started to whine about how this would slow up my trip and also cost me money, of which I, being a college student, had a lot of, right! Man, was I lucky. From the impact of the snow on the embankment that was created by the snowplow, it dented the back fender on the driver's side of my car. However, since I told myself to relax while this moment of despair happened, I was okay.

Well, the car I had just passed stopped to help me. The young woman got out of her car and asked me if I was okay. Even though I heard her, I did not say anything at first; however, I did whine about my situation inwardly. While I whimpered on about what just happened to me, she asked me again if I was okay. This time I said I was, but stated that my car was dented, and then I thanked her because she stopped to help. She asked me if I needed to get to a phone, for she did not have a truck to help get me out. I somewhat ignored what she offered and continued in my thoughts of what to do. She asked again if there was anything she could do, and as I tried to avoid the tears from my eyes, I asked her for a hug. She smiled and said sure.

After we hugged, another woman came along and asked if anyone needed a phone. I asked her if she had a cellular phone and she said yes. She told me I could use it to call a wrecker. After I called the wrecker, I offered to give some money to the woman with the car phone, but she wouldn't take it. I thanked her and got out of her car. The other woman who stood there while I called 911 gave me another hug. The two women asked me if they needed to stay while I waited, and I told them I was okay and they didn't need to stay. I thanked both women for their help and went back to my car.

Shortly after they left, the wrecker service came and pulled me out of the field for a small fee, and I went home for the weekend and made it to Katrina's baptism on time.

The reason I felt it was important to share this little story with you was to share a moment in time that could have been an unpleasant one for my body, but since I told myself to relax when my body wanted to do the opposite, I was able to come out of the situation okay. And even though my car was hurt a little, my body wasn't.

In conclusion, the lesson here is to relax when confronted with uncomfortable situations, for it is at times like this when relaxation is needed the most.

The Price of Jewels

Spring of 1998

THE NIGHT SKY WAS filled with stars and the most beautiful full moon Emma had ever seen. She wrapped her arms around Naldy and gave him a gentle kiss on the lips. He smiled and whispered in her ear to be careful. The two embraced for a long moment before Emma turned and ran toward the beach in Panama City, Florida. The ocean water was calm that night as she walked toward the rocky area that traveled out into the ocean. The beach itself wasn't very big because of the rocks that covered it. The breeze off the water felt nice on her face as she walked, and the ocean water brushed across her bare feet as she walked closer to the rocks where the boat was.

The rocks that led to the boat had a slight incline, which made it difficult to walk on. After she reached the top, her foot slipped, and she almost fell. She quickly regained her composure and slowly climbed down the rocks until she reached the water around ten feet below. She slid into the water and swam into the cavern-like structure she was just on top of. The boat was anchored to a rock that protruded from the wall. It was a nice location to hide the Sport-

Craft boat, for it was hidden. She carefully pulled herself into the boat and grabbed the duffel bag located under the steering column. Emma opened it and pulled out a towel and some dry clothes. She took off the wet clothes from her lanky body, dried herself with the towel, and wrapped it around her long blond hair. She put on the dry clothes, took the towel off, and pulled an envelope off the steering column.

It was already two months since the robbery, and it was one of the smoothest jobs ever done. The only thing left to do was to get the jewels. Emma unsealed the letter and found it was only several miles to the cemetery. No one suspected her as the thief except for the town sheriff, and she really didn't need to worry about him.

She was sad about the sheriff because she liked him and thought he liked her too. He with his average stocky body and a face anyone could love. She was slightly taller than him, but that didn't matter. She thought about the scar he had two inches above the genitals. He told her it was a war wound from earlier years but would not tell her the specifics. He would just say he was lucky it didn't hit his little babies. She would laugh and grab them gently.

Mm, she thought, *it was nice.* He never realized she was with him because of the jewels. He thought she was in love with him. She was good. One of the best manipulators around she felt. She untied the boat and began her journey.

The letter said she had several miles to travel before she would reach the cemetery. There was a dock she could tie the boat to on the outside of it. The still waters and full moon soothed her as she drifted slowly downstream. The sound of crickets along with an occasional owl and the frogs harmonized together as the boat progressed. Her decision to keep the engine off helped her to travel unnoticed. It was a very serene way to travel. Emma gazed up at the stars while she floated downstream, and for a moment, she inhaled the beauty of the nature that surrounded her. It was close to midnight when she found the cemetery and docked the boat by the edge of it.

Emma sat there in the boat for a moment and listened for any strange noises. There were none. She pulled the letter out of her pocket and the flashlight out of the duffel bag. She shined the light on the letter and read it more carefully.

> Emma, no time to waste, go downstream approximately seven miles or so until you reach the pier by the cemetery.
>
> Once you get there walk onto the cemetery grounds until you reach the diamond-shaped tombstone in the center of the graveyard. Reach down by the base of the stone and retrieve the letter. It will explain where you need to go next.

Now that she read the rest of the letter, she knew something was wrong. As she walked to the designated tombstone, she listened for any strange noises. The shadows that filled the cemetery gave it an eerie look and feel. Not just because it was a cemetery, but because of the type of tombstones on it.

She walked onto the graveyard grounds and noticed a tombstone in the shape of a man; only it held the head with its hands.

Weird, she thought and started to get a closer look when suddenly she noticed a gigantic diamond-shaped tombstone right in the center of the graveyard. Its size pulled her toward it. She could not believe it. It was about ten feet high and six feet wide at its girdle (center). She was amazed at how detailed the stone was. She could not find a flaw on it anywhere. No chips or scratches. She was impressed at the workmanship of this stone. It resembled a diamond perfectly. Except it wasn't real. It looked like it was made from zircon.

Unbelievable. Why did my brother feel he needed to be so mysterious about this? This is such a strange place. He better have a good reason for it, she thought.

She looked at the pavilion (base) of the stone and read it: "Founded in 1818."

"Mm," she said as she jerked her head to one side. "This place was founded in 1818. I guess it isn't a cemetery then. If it's not a cemetery, what is it?" As she said this, she admired the facets (details) of this particular stone. She looked at the pavilion part of the stone and noticed a piece of paper next to the stone with a small stick shoved through it. She pulled the stick out of the ground and picked up the letter. It read: "Just under the willow tree, you will find thy precious gifts."

"Under the willow tree, mm, that's right! Just under the willow tree at Kentucky's Limestone Cave." The Limestone Cave was a place he and her frequented in their childhood years.

She thought back to when she was fifteen and her brother was seventeen. They gave an old man money to buy them a couple of bottles of liquor. He bought them one bottle of brandy and one bottle of whiskey. They took it to the cave and drank over half of the whiskey. They were so drunk, it was difficult for the two of them to walk home. It was so bad, the two of them had to lean on each other for the mile walk to the house.

Once they got to the house, Ruby fell to his knees and puked all over the front porch. Emma fell with him and landed right in the vomit. The smell revolted her, and she vomited. They both lay there on the front porch until their parents came home from the dinner engagement they had earlier that night. When their parents saw the two of them on the porch in the mess, they just sighed. Their dad picked them both up at the same time and took them to the side of the house to wash them off with the hose. Emma vaguely remembered her brother's red face. What she did remember was a parent who held his temper as he told them how they would pay for it in the morning, and they did. Oh, how they paid for it the next day. Emma couldn't even get out of bed. Ruby tried but was unsuccessful. He just fell on the floor and stayed there for hours. When he finally did get up, his face was still red from the night before, and their dad said he was a real gem, like a ruby. The name stayed with him. A week later, they went back into the cave to get the other bottle and gave it to a bum on the street.

Suddenly, she began to feel uneasy and stood up to look around. There was something really weird about the terrain she stood on. Not that she didn't think it was odd before; it just became more apparent now. She realized there was a headless tombstone on each corner. One faced east, west, north, and south, and there was an elf on the right side of the north tombstone. The diamond was right in the center, and when the full moon shined on it, the shadow it created pointed right at a house one hundred yards away.

She wondered why things were arranged the way they were in this cemetery or whatever it was. It seemed to be a distance from the road and was secluded by means of pine trees as well as some oak. The pine trees were arranged in a horseshoe way with the cemetery planted inside the shoe. This seemed very strange to Emma. She began to question everything. Why were the trees planted where they were? Why the shadow on the house and why was there a house on this land? There was also what was written on the diamond, which made her question whether or not the land she stood on was a cemetery or a landmark. She felt she needed more time to investigate, but it was late, and she needed some rest. She decided to put her inquisitorial mind to rest for the night and went to the boat. As she walked, she looked at the note.

"Just under the old willow tree." She smiled and thought about what a clever brother she had. He took jewels to a place they frequented when the two were children.

She wondered for a moment if it was safe to go there anymore. The tree was the landmark that identified the place. It was located right above the cave's entrance and sat with many other pine, oak, and willow trees. The secret place itself was a cave. The uniqueness of this specific cave was it was hidden from eyes' view because of the shrubs that covered the entrance.

The way Emma and Ruby found it was an experience in itself. Ruby climbed on the willow to show off his manliness to Emma and dared her to climb it too. As he climbed up the branches, he stepped on a weak one and slid down the tree and ended up in the shrubs at the bottom. When he tried to get free from it, he fell back into the cavern. It had been many years since she had been to that cave, though the memories of it were still very strong. After these thoughts, she crawled into the boat, grabbed a sleeping bag, and went to sleep. She drifted off to sleep while the sounds of nature harmonized around her.

The morning sun began to rise when suddenly, *crackle, crackle, crackle.* Emma shot up from the boat. "What was that?" She thought about the piece of paper and became more worried about her brother. She quickly untied the boat and let the current push it downstream. She watched to make sure no one could see her as she drifted away from the cemetery. After a couple of miles, she started the engine and headed toward town.

* * * * *

It was a little past five when she arrived at the limestone caves in Kentucky. The cave was about a mile from where she used to live. She reassured herself that no one else could have explored the cave because of how well it was hidden.

When she saw the willow tree, it was split in half, right down the middle, and some of the thick heavy branches covered the entrance of the cave.

"A person could climb up that branch and look into the cave," she said as she walked closer. "It doesn't look like the whole entrance is closed off though." She continued as her mind went back in time. There was a crevice about two hundred feet into the cave where Emma and Ruby used to hide their little treasures. Carefully, she climbed up the broken branch until she reached the entrance. Emma lay on her stomach and wrapped her arms around the branch and swung herself into the cave. She slid right on her buttocks and scratched her arm as she slid in.

"Ouch," she said.

The cool dampness in the air made her shiver, and she slowly stood up to listen more closely. There was silence all around her except for the sound of water that dripped from the cave's ceiling. It was then she remembered how the cave affected her. The damp cool air along with the *drip, drip, drip* of the water made her feel cold and uneasy inside. Only this time she felt it even more strongly. She stood silently for a moment and suddenly realized it was light in there.

Since there was nowhere for light to enter the cave, Emma became nervous and stooped down on her knees. She listened for any kind of noise. *Drip, drip, drip.* Her heart began to beat faster, and she decided to walk into the cavern toward the light.

The cavern ceiling was about five feet above her head, and its width was around twenty-five feet. As she walked closer to the light it became colder. She shivered from the dampness in the air and pulled out the .32 caliber pistol that was tucked in the back of her jeans. The cave circled to the right slightly, and as she started to walk around it, she noticed a lantern on a rod stuck out of the cavern's wall and there was no one around. Just the lantern.

Emma felt someone had to be there but saw no one. She heard a noise and quickly scrunched down. *Drip, drip, drip.* She took a deep breath, stood up, and with the lantern in hand, continued to walk forward. She walked to the crevice and looked inside when suddenly there was another noise! *Crunch, crunch.*

"What was that?" she whispered and set the lantern down. Cautiously, she walked further into the cave and knelt down on the floor where the cave split. *Crunch, crunch,* her breath became faster, and her body started to quiver. She listened to the footsteps which came closer and closer. Her heart started to beat faster, and she wondered what on earth she was supposed to do. Very few people knew about this cave. At least this was what she wanted to think, but she really didn't know. She took a deep breath and thought for a moment about who it could be. Then through a process of elimination, she decided it was her brother.

"Yes, it must be." Then she remembered the graveyard and the noise she heard in the morning. Suddenly, there was a light on the cavern's wall where it turned not far from where she stood. *Oh my god!* she thought. She took the revolver and pointed it in the direction of the noise. The footsteps came closer and closer until the figure stood five feet in front of her. Sweat began to fall off her cheeks, and her hands began to tremble as she cocked the gun.

"Emma?" said a familiar voice. "Emma, are you there? It's me, Ruby."

Emma simultaneously disarmed the gun and dropped her arms. A heavy sigh followed as she stood up. She was grateful it was her brother and ran into his arms. He reciprocated and told her to calm down.

"How did you know it was me?" asked Emma.

"Because the lantern wasn't on the rod where I left it and I knew you were on your way, remember?" he said.

Emma looked into his hazel eyes.

"I almost shot you, Ruby."

"But you didn't, Emma. You *did* notice the tree outside, didn't you?" he said sarcastically.

"That in itself would stop a person. Besides, who else knows about this place?"

"Good point, Ruby. So talk to me, like what happened?"

Ruby gently grabbed Emma by the arm and suggested they go back outside where it was warmer. She agreed since she was so cold from the damp air. He grabbed the lantern with the other hand, and the two of them crawled out of the cave. Once they were out of the cave, Ruby started to talk.

"I have some bad news for you, Emma."

"What do you mean you've got bad news?"

"Well, it's about Naldy. He is kind of umm, well, dead!"

"*Dead?*"

"Yes, he had a car accident. He passed someone on a curb and met another car head-on." Her mind went back to the beach when they said goodbye, and a tear fell down her face. She thought about his gentle touch and how he made her feel comforted whenever she felt blue. She glanced at Ruby with a questionable look as tears fell from her face.

"Was it a setup? I mean, Christ, Ruby, this does not sound right to me. Naldy wouldn't pass on a curve. He is much smarter than that. Now tell me what's going on."

"Things have become a little complicated, Emma. We accidentally took a very valuable stone."

"Ruby, we took all of them. Wasn't that the purpose? To get *all* of them?"

"Well, yeah, but we took a very valuable one that belonged to a drug lord who had it put on display. And I might add, he knows who we are because the sheriff told him."

"You mean the sheriff works for him?" she said with a look of surprise on her face. There was a moment of silence before Ruby started to talk again.

"Well, actually, Emma, I think he is the drug lord—I mean, he probably is." There was silence for a moment before Ruby started to talk again.

"The drug lord wants us to take his precious jewel to his headquarters, and his headquarters is at the cemetery where you got my note from." Emma put her hands on her forehead and released a heavy sigh then she slowly dropped down to the ground while tears fell from her face.

"Naldy's dead. How can this be? I just saw him a couple of days ago." The tears continued to fall from her face as she sat on the ground; the realization of Naldy's death had her in hysterics. Ruby sat down next to her and put his arms around her.

"I'm sorry, Emma. I felt I had to tell you." She pressed her cheek against his shoulder and cried. Suddenly, she stopped and jumped up.

"That's his headquarters?" she said with a stern voice. "I don't think it's a cemetery, Ruby. It looked more like a landmark of some sort. There was an inscription on the diamond that said it was founded in 1818. Something is very fishy here."

"Emma, don't let your imagination run wild here. I just don't want anything to go wrong."

"Ruby, it just doesn't make sense to me for him to be a drug lord and a cop. But I guess what better cover could a drug lord have than the one he has chosen? He protects himself that way. It just pisses me off. Now this will slow up our plans. Christ, first Naldy's dead and now we have to take a jewel to someone who claims to be a drug lord."

"Look, Emma, I just think we need to be safe and make sure of things. Besides, once we drop off the jewel, we are out of here and on the plane to Jamaica."

"I guess you're right. It just doesn't make sense for Naldy to pass on a curve. Now back to business, Ruby, is the so-called cemetery really his headquarters? Because it was like the strangest one I have ever seen. There were only a few tombstones there. Unless the house is the headquarters."

"Emma, the headquarters is underneath."

"Underneath?"

"Yes, apparently all you have to do is shake the elf's right hand and the entrance to the hideout opens."

"Do you know where the entrance is?"

"Not really, I guess we will find that out when we return the jewel."

"I still think something is fishy here." At the end of the conversation, Emma felt exhausted from all the new information she received and forgot to ask where the jewels were. Her heart was heavy from the loss of her love and the deception from the sheriff. Ruby pulled out a couple of sleeping bags he had stashed behind the shrubs by the cave. He tossed one to Emma, and they camped out by the cave for the night.

* * * * *

At daybreak the two of them woke up, coiled up the sleeping bags, and walked back to the cave's entrance. "Why are we going back to the cave, Ruby?"

"To get the jewels. I found a different place to hide them." Ruby climbed up the branch of the broken tree, lay on the branch, and swung himself in. Emma did the same, and once they entered the cave, Ruby grabbed the lantern, and the two walked into the cave. They passed the crevice where Emma thought the jewels were and continued until they reached the area where the cave split which was five feet farther. Ruby grabbed Emma's hand and walked into the opening on the right. As they walked, the ceiling became lower and lower and the circumference became smaller too. It got to the point where the two of them crawled side by side and above them were only inches.

After they crawled around twenty feet, Ruby stopped. By this time, they were both wet from all the water on the cave's floor. Emma became impatient and asked Ruby to hurry. Just as she said this Ruby moved an oblong rock from the wall and reached his hand into the open area and pulled out a bag and opened it. He reached in and grabbed the diamond that was mixed in with the other jewels. It was shaped like the tombstone at the cemetery and was one of the biggest stones in the bag. As a matter of fact, it was the only diamond in the bag. The rest were sapphires, rubies, and emeralds. They both looked at the diamond for a moment, then Ruby put it in a jeweler's bag and shoved it in his pocket. He closed the bag and told Emma it was time to leave.

* * * * *

It was early afternoon when they arrived in Panama City, Florida. The warmth of the sun made the ride there a comfortable one. Ruby parked the motorcycle by an old diner off the waterfront and the two of them went into a gun store to purchase a .45 caliber and ammunition. "I hope we don't need to use a gun, Ruby."

"I don't either, Emma, but we have to be safe."

"What time do we need to go to the cemetery?"

"After dark when the shadows come out."

"Is it important for us to see the shadows, Ruby?"

"Very. The shadows will guide us to the opening of the hideout."

Emma thought back to when she was in the cemetery and grabbed her brother's arm. "How do you know all this?"

"It was written in the letter I received a couple of days before you arrived."

"Ruby, why didn't you tell me this earlier?"

"I felt I gave you enough information at the time. I didn't want to stress your mind any more than I already had."

"This sounds like a setup to me, Ruby."

"Emma, I know this sounds unbelievable, but you have to trust me."

"Ruby, you're my brother, of course I trust you. I just feel a little uneasy about the whole thing."

"Me too. That's why I bought another gun."

"I think we could hide the jewels. We could put them into a waterproof bag and anchor them off one of the pier's poles by the cemetery."

"Sounds good to me, Emma. Now let's get started."

Emma and Ruby went to the local diner on Fifth called Sunshine Inn and ate the special of the day called "grits-n-egg." Grits was a southern specialty that was known to fill a person for most of the day.

* * * * *

By the time they reached the cemetery, it was dark. Ruby tied the boat to the dock, then tied the bag of jewels to the pier and dropped them into the water. The two of them got out of the boat and proceeded to the graveyard. This night the moon did not light up the cemetery. As the two of them walked to the elf, the sound of the crickets seemed to cry a different sound than the one Emma heard when she was there before. The two walked cautiously to the elf and stood there for a moment. Emma knelt down to look at the elf more closely. It had a smile on its face. She looked at her brother then back to the elf and sighed.

"Ruby, I hope you're right about this because something feels really strange about it. I mean I trust you and everything, but we are here at night, just the two of us, and we have no idea what will happen when we find this hideout. Ruby, it could be a setup," she said with emphasis. "We do have the option to leave, you know."

"I know, Emma, but we both have guns and I don't think you want to look over your shoulder for the rest of your life!"

"Good point, Ruby. I knew there was a reason I wanted you to help with this."

"Yeah, I know we kind of balance things out between the two of us, don't we?" He looked at her and smiled.

Emma smiled and nodded back. When the shadow reached its highest point, Emma shook the hand of the elf. When she released her hand, the tip of the shadow reached right behind the house, and there was a sudden vibration on the ground. Emma got up from the ground, and the two of them stood there for a moment and watched as the diamond opened up. They just stood there in silence and watched.

"Unbelievable," said Emma, "Can you believe it, Ruby? And the way the diamond opened up at the widest part. Christ, I never noticed a crack in it when I looked at it the other night. How clever." They looked at each other and began to walk toward the structure. When they reached it, the two of them looked inside and then at each other. All they could see was a flat surface that a person could stand on. They both had an expression of confusion on their faces until Emma finally said, "Let's go inside the diamond and see what happens."

They both climbed in and stood for a moment then suddenly the flat surface dropped open, and the two of them started to slide down a shoot. Emma wrapped her arms around Ruby as the two of them slid. "Hang on to me, Ruby."

Suddenly, they were on the floor right in front of two feet. They both looked up, and there was the sheriff with a smile on his face. Emma looked at him. "I thought I took care of you!" The sheriff looked at her and smiled.

"I know, but you were wrong. The bottle of gin you gave me I gave to the man you had your arms around at the beach. When I saw the two of you kiss, I thought it only appropriate to give him the bottle. I followed him to the hotel and had the busboy take it to his room shortly after he arrived. He thought it was a gift from you. I sent it to him with a little note. It was such a sweet note. Shall I recite it for you? Yes, I think I will. 'Honey, I thought of you when I saw this bottle of gin, hope you enjoy. Love, Emma.' Such a sweet thing for you to do, Emma."

"You bastard!"

"That's not a nice way to talk to your future husband."

"Future husband! I don't think so."

"Now, Emma, didn't we share some good times, you and me?"

"I only used you, you idiot!"

"I kind of figured that out. However, I know you felt something for me, for I could see it in your eyes."

She looked at him with painful eyes and then her face softened and her gaze shifted downward to the floor.

"If Naldy drank the alcohol in his room, why did he leave the hotel?"

"After Naldy went to his room, I waited a while and then called him on the phone. I muffled my voice and told him there was a boat accident and we needed someone to come identify the body. I told him the Coast Guard found a note in the woman's pocket with his name and the hotel he was at on it. It also had the hotel's phone number on it.

"When he left, I went to his room to make sure he drank some of the gin. He apparently had a few. I took the bottle, left the hotel, and went where I sent him. He only made it to Corners Bend. It's a pretty sharp curve, and he must have cramped or something, for he took it wide and was in the other lane long enough to meet another car head-on. The good thing here is that he hit an older car with an older man in it who had no relation alive to be concerned with."

Emma just stood there in shock. She couldn't believe what she just heard. She looked at Ruby who looked a little surprised himself. Then Emma looked back at the sheriff, and a tear fell from her face.

"Is there really a drug lord?"

"No, dear, it was just the only way to get you here. If I would have written who I really was in the letter to your brother, you might not have come and I would not get the diamond. By the way, where is it?" Ruby reached into his pocket and pulled out the bag with the diamond in it. He held it in his hand and looked at the sheriff.

"How do we know we can trust you after you have this precious stone?"

"You have no other choice. Besides, the two of you are thieves, so I don't feel the need to worry about it. Since it would incriminate you to do so."

The sheriff winked at them as he said this. Ruby tossed the diamond to him.

"You've got a point, Sheriff. One question though. Why is this diamond so important to you?" The sheriff looked at the diamond carefully with an eyepiece.

"This jewel was found by my great-grandfather. Did you notice the date inscribed by the diamond-shaped stone above us?"

They both nodded.

"Well, he found this diamond in 1818. It was also the time he built the structure above us. It's not really a cemetery, but more like a landmark. He became a very rich man from this land. There was so much money in it, he decided to build this strange place to protect it from the greedy hands of other explorers. You would be surprised at the rock formations still untouched here. It's unbelievable.

"This place has been passed down from generation to generation. Now I own it, and when I have children, they will inherit it. That's where you come in, Emma. In time, after you have healed from the death of Naldy, I will come and look for you. Hopefully, you will understand that I love and also forgive you for what you tried to do. I felt you did it out of necessity. Anyway, I feel we are even since Naldy is dead. I am optimistic about it."

Emma just stood there with a blank look on her face. Ruby looked at her and then the sheriff. "Now what?" The sheriff reached into his pocket and pulled out two tickets and gave them to Ruby.

"Here are two first class tickets to Jamaica. With the jewels you have, you should be able to live very nicely there. You should also be able to cash in those jewels there with no problem. There is a man by the name of Razor Blade. He will be able to help you sell the merchandise." He looked over at Emma with a gentle look on his face and smiled.

"In time, I will come visit you. I hope your wounds will be healed, and you are ready for me. We shared some good times, you and me. I hope we will be able to do that again."

"I think you are too optimistic, Sheriff. You killed Naldy and you think I will forgive you. I don't know why you think I would want to be with you." Emma looked at him with angry eyes.

"Emma, we should leave before you do something foolish. We have the other jewels and now we have two tickets to leave the country. I think we should just leave."

"Okay, Ruby, I'll deal with this later." She looked at the sheriff. "Don't you even think for a minute I will want you. Do you understand me, Sheriff?"

"You're upset right now, Emma, give it time. I *am* right around the corner, and soon enough I will come for you. You can count on it."

"I look forward to the day," she said in an angered tone.

* * * * *

While Emma and Ruby were flying to Jamaica, Emma reflected back to everything that happened. Earlier on this adventure, she thought she was the best. Later she found out she was outsmarted by the man she thought she killed. She really didn't know what to think of the sheriff. It was apparent he could have gotten rid of both of them. Yet he didn't, and she could clearly see why he didn't, but she didn't understand how he felt she would want him after he killed her boyfriend.

"Ruby, I don't understand why the sheriff thinks I will want him. I don't want to love him. I want to kill him for what he did to Naldy, and when he comes to see me, he is in for a big surprise."

"First, he has to find us, Emma. Let's just leave all that behind us."

"You're right, Ruby, it is all behind us now." She looked at her brother and smiled, and then she looked out the airplane window and thought about her next move.

The End

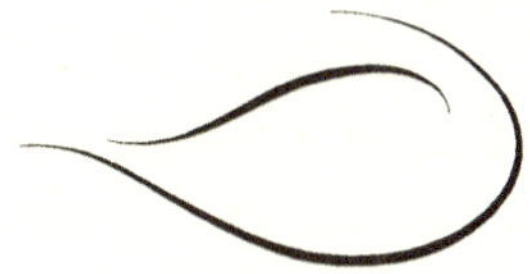

All You Have to Do

Spring of 1998

THIS STORY BEGINS IN Madison, Wisconsin. It is about a young woman who finds out she has a weakness in school when dealing with her learning abilities. She is a junior in college and has just recently moved to Madison to finish her college tenure. Shortly after her arrival in Madison, fall was in the air, and the semester began. Initially, she felt great about school and was amazed at how easy some of her classes were. She felt her schooling at Madison would be a breeze—well, at least initially she did. That is, she felt confident until it was time for the tests. There was something about tests with her. And when she took the first tests at the beginning of the semester, she felt she did well on two of the three she took. After she received her grades, she called her mom, and lights fade off the speaker and turn onto the stage for act 1.

Act 1 scene 1

LESLEY, *on the phone*: Mom, I failed three tests this week and each grade came from a different class. (*Pause.*) I know why I failed one of the tests, but the other two I thought I did well on. *(Heavy sigh)*.

(There is a pause for a couple of seconds).

LESLEY: Thanks, Mom, I know I just moved here and it takes time to become adjusted. However, I've never done this poorly in college before. I'm like a junior and all of a sudden, I just out-of-the-blue fail three tests. *(Pause for a few seconds)*.

LESLEY, *with a sad tone in her voice*: Mom, you've already told me there is a time of adjustment after a move. It's just I thought I did extremely well on one of those tests and I bombed it with flying colors. *(Pause for a few seconds while a tear falls down her face)*. All I know is that this is not the best way to start a semester. *(Pause for a few seconds.)*

LESLEY: Thanks for the moral support, Mom. I'll talk to you later. Love you too. *(Pause.)* Bye. *(Hangs up the phone, sighs, then says out loud.)* I guess it's time to make an appointment with the McBurney Center. *(Gets out the phone book and looks up the number for the McBurney Center and dials the number.)* Hello, my name is Lesley, and I would like to make an appointment to see a counselor. *(Pause)*. As soon as possible. *(Pause.)* Yes, I'm a student. *(Pause.)* Bring my ID with me, okay. Friday at 3:00 p.m. That would be fine. Thank you very much. Goodbye. *(Spotlight on her as she looks into space.)* How could this happen? What does it mean? *(She slowly lowers her head and brings her hands up to her face and covers it. Lights fade as she does this.)*

End of scene
1st talent

Act 1 Scene 2

Mcburney Center. This is a place where special students go to receive accommodations for his or her special needs.

LESLEY: I have an appointment at three with Mary.

RECEP: Please sit down and I will tell her you are here. *(Young girl goes to sit down, and within a minute, the counselor comes out of her office.)*

MARY: What can I help you with?

LESLEY: I'm here because I did poorly on three tests. Two of which I studied for extensively.

MARY: What about the third one?

LESLEY: Well, I didn't really study for that one because I felt I would do well on the third one.

MARY: Why did you think that?

LESLEY: Since the class was a physical fitness program and I am athletic, I felt I would know all the information needed for the test.

MARY: Well, that's confidence.

LESLEY, *snorting*: I don't know if I would call it confidence. Arrogance, maybe, but not confidence.

MARY: What is it you want me to do for you?

LESLEY: I was hoping you could help me find out why this has happened to me.

MARY: Are you willing to take some tests?

LESLEY: Will it help me find the answer to my dilemma? *(She looks at Mary with a sad questionable look.)*

MARY: What it will do is tell you where your weaknesses are in the scholastic arena.

LESLEY: What happens after I find out what my weaknesses are?

MARY: It depends upon your needs.

LESLEY: Could you give me an example?

MARY: There are notetakers for some students and also extra time on tests. There are also alternative test taking and more, but first, we have to take the tests before we know which ones would apply to your situation.

LESLEY: Oh, really?

MARY: First, we have to make an appointment for you to be screened by one of our psychiatrists. After the screening, the psychiatrist will recommend some tests for you to take. The results will inform you where your weakness lies. *(Mary calls to make an appointment and while she is doing this Lesley looks toward the audience with a distant look on her face. As if she were somewhere else. The curtain close.)*

End of scene

Act 1 Scene 3

Scene starts in the psychology office. Both the psychologist and Lesley are sitting. There is a loveseat against the wall next to the door. In the corner next to the loveseat is an end table with a lamp on it. Next to the lamp is a tall chair.
   There is a desk by the window and a shelf with books in it.

JOHN: What is it I can help you with?

LESLEY: I failed three tests in three different classes and would like to know why.

JOHN: Have you ever taken any kind of psychological test before?

LESLEY: Once in Texas after back surgery, I had to take a test to see if I would be able to handle college.

JOHN: Do you remember the results?

LESLEY: *(She looks at the floor, then back at him.)* Basically, the psychiatrist told me college would be difficult for me.

JOHN: How did you feel about that?

LESLEY, *putting her favored hand on her face with her index finger on her mouth. As she does this, she looks off to the right and thinks for a moment:* I felt he did not know me well enough to make such a claim.

JOHN, *sitting back in his chair and contemplating for a moment:* What I want to do is set an appointment for you with one of our psychologists. *(Pause.)* She will help make the arrangements for you to take the tests.

LESLEY: How soon?

JOHN: First, I need to assign you a psychologist. *(He picks up the phone and dials the number)*

LESLEY, *as he dials the number and with a questionable look*: Can we start right away? *(He signals her to wait.)*

JOHN: Hello, Sharron, I have a student here that I would like for you to see. *(Pause).* This Wednesday? *(Pause.)* At three o'clock. *(He looks up at Lesley to see if the time suits her, and Lesley nods her head.)* Three o'clock would be fine. *(Pause.)* Her name is Lesley. Goodbye.

LESLEY: So I guess that's it until Wednesday?

JOHN: Yes.

LESLEY, *getting up to leave*: Thank you for your time.

JOHN: You're welcome, and remember your appointment.

LESLEY: I'll be there with bells hopping. *(She says lightly to make the situation lighter).*

JOHN: Bells hopping?

LESLEY: It's an expression used to make a situation lighter than it feels.

JOHN: Mm. *(He ponders what he just heard.)* Interesting.

LESLEY, *smiling*: Bye, Doc.

JOHN: Bye. Bells hopping—I'm going to ask my secretary if she understands it.

End of scene

Act 1 Scene 4

The scene begins in the psychologist's office.

SHARRON: Please sit down. *(Gestures toward chair with hand.)* Now what is it I can help you with?

LESLEY, *looking at the audience*: Like how many times do I have to say this? *(Then looks back. Sharron does not sway her vision away from Lesley.)* I'm here because I failed three tests in three different classes and would like to know why.

SHARRON: Oh, really? Does it bother you to talk about it?

LESLEY, *looking at her with an expression of disbelief, as if the psychologist didn't hear what she said*: I don't know, maybe. *(As she shakes her head slightly back and forth, from left to right.)*

SHARRON: Do you want to talk about it?

LESLEY: (*Her movements are in disbelief as she talks and she looks as if she is annoyed by it.*) I don't know. You know, it's like here I am in my thirties, and all of a sudden out of the blue, I find out I might have a weakness. (*Looks down at the floor.*) No, wait, that's not what it's called. It's called a learning disability. I don't really know what to think about it. I have come to one conclusion, and that would be to face it. (*Pause.*) Whatever *it* may be. (*She said sarcastically.*)

SHARRON, *smiling*: That's the right attitude.

LESLEY: Easy for you to say.

SHARRON: (continuing as if she did not hear what Lesley said.) The tests will give you an idea of where your difficulty is. After you take the tests, you will be able to deal with the problem by concentrating on your strengths and using them to compensate for your weakness.

LESLEY: Just that simple?

SHARRON: No, it will take you time to learn the new system.

LESLEY: Do you teach me this new system, whatever it may be?

SHARRON: No, you do. For instance, if you need flash cards to study from you would have to write them up. However, if you need a notetaker, we can help you with that.

LESLEY: When do I take the first test?

SHARRON: First you would need to fill out this questionnaire. It asks very personal questions and you need to answer them honestly. (*Hands Lesley the paper.*)

LESLEY, *taking the paper and looking at the heading*: Drug and alcohol history?

SHARRON: Yes.

LESLEY: (*She says in disbelief.*) What does this questionnaire have to do with my weakness?

SHARRON: This will help us understand your situation better.

LESLEY: (*Looks at her in disbelief.*) How could this help to understand my situation better?

SHARRON: It tells us if you have any problems with drugs and alcohol.

LESLEY: These are very personal questions. Can anyone look at them?

Sharron: No, in order for someone to read your records, the individual would have to get written permission from you.

Lesley: Good to know.

Sharron: The psychologist who will give you the tests is Robert. Is Monday at nine and Tuesday at three thirty okay for you?

Lesley: *(Looks at her appointment book.)* Sure.

Sharron: It will take a week before the results are in, and then I will see you on the following Tuesday at three thirty.

Lesley: Sounds fine. I will see you in a couple of weeks. *(Lights fade.)*

End of scene
2nd talent

Act 2: Scene 1

Lesley has completed the tests she needed to and is now sitting in Sharron's office ready to hear the results.

Lesley: So what were the results?

Sharron: The tests show you have a weakness in your ability to learn vocally.

Lesley: What! *(She says with a shocked look!)*

Sharron: It means when you are in the classroom listening to the teacher, you are not getting out of the lesson what the other students are. Something happens to the information when it enters your memory.

Lesley: What? *(She says with a questionable look.)* I understand the teacher when I am in the classroom.

Sharron: This may be so, but when you leave the classroom, what do you take with you?

Lesley: Well, when I leave the class, I feel I'm doing well since I understood everything the teacher said while in class.

Sharron: What about when you bring information back from your memory?

Lesley: When I take a test, I get real nervous because of what happens to me when I look at the exam.

SHARRON: What happens?

LESLEY: First, I look at the questions and my mind goes blank. Then my heart starts to beat a little faster and my body begins to shake. I try to relax by breathing and telling myself to relax, but when I look at the questions again, I am still unable to place the material in the right context. Especially with multiple-choice questions. I can rationalize every answer to be right. Which of course, makes me a little more nervous. I'm usually the last one in the room too. Circling answers as quickly as possible before the time runs out. Hoping in my desperation my guesses are right. And by this time, my brain is drained, and I leave the classroom with a heavy heart while I fight the tears from—well, let's just say it is a weak moment for me. I don't look forward to the day when I get the test back either. For I know I will receive something that only makes me feel stupid and I wonder what is wrong with me. To work so hard, I just don't get it. *(She looks up at Sharron with a very sad look on her face and watery eyes.)* Does this mean I'm stupid?

SHARRON: No, it doesn't mean you're stupid. It just means you learn differently than others.

LESLEY: I still don't understand.

SHARRON: Okay, when you are in class and listen to the lecture and feel you understand everything, well, something happens to the information when it goes through the memory process. You may understand what the professor is saying. However, it doesn't have anything to peg itself on when it goes into the memory and therefore gets lost. *(Pause.)* We also found out your ability to learn visually was ranked in the superior range. As a matter of fact, Robert said your ability with visuals knocked his socks off. He said he has never seen a score that high before, and he has given this test to many people. We also feel this is why you are able to handle college, for your vocal scores were rather low.

LESLEY, *looking at the audience*: I thought he was wearing shoes. *(Shakes her head)* Really, is this supposed to make me feel better? You tell me I have a superior intellect yet I don't learn the way school is taught. For some reason, it doesn't make me feel better or smarter either. (*Snorts.*) It sure doesn't feel like I have a superior intellect when I look at the results on my tests. Boy, is this ever a big pill to swallow.

SHARRON: There was something else.

LESLEY: (*Heavy sigh.*) There's more?

SHARRON: Yes, you also have an anxiety problem.

LESLEY: Great! The cause of that problem would be school. I call it test anxiety. I never look forward to taking those multiple scramble-your-brain type tests. Like it really matters whether or not a person is able to take a test or not in real life. (*Pause.*) How did you figure this out?

SHARRON: We compared the scores with the ones you gave us from Texas. (*She shows Lesley the two scores on a scale.*) The scores of the test you took here have skyrocketed in comparison to the earlier one. Because the difference is so large, it tells us you have an anxiety problem. (*Pause. Lesley looks exhausted and there is a distant look in her face.*) Lesley, you are an intelligent woman. These test results are only a small part of what the brain is able to do.

LESLEY: Yeah, right! You apparently did not listen to what you just told me. First, you tell me I don't learn the way school is taught, then you say I have a superior intellect followed by the statement I have an anxiety problem. (*Lesley shakes her head and sighs*.) So tell me: if I have such a superior intellect, why is school so difficult?

SHARRON: Because you need visual cues.

LESLEY: Visual cues?

SHARRON: Yes, visual cues. You see, Lesley, your visual is in the superior range, which means you need visual cues to peg the information to.

LESLEY: Great! What next?

SHARRON: We give the information to Mary, so she can get a program started. (*She calls Mary to set the appointment.*) Hello, Mary, can you see Lesley at 10:00 a.m. tomorrow? (*Looks at Lesley*

who shakes her head yes.) You can? Great, goodbye. (*She looks at Lesley.*) Mary will see you in the morning.
LESLEY: Thanks for your promptness.

End of scene
3rd Talent

Act 2 Scene 2

Lesley is at the bar with her friend. There is a bar, bartender (Bt), stools, and a few extras.

BT: What can I get you two to drink?
JERRY: I'll have a scotch and water, and the lady will have a?
LESLEY: Coors light. *(Looks at Jerry)* What a day it has been.
JERRY: What happened?
LESLEY: I found out I have a learning disability.
JERRY: Really? In what way?
LESLEY: Vocally.
JERRY: Vocally?
LESLEY: Yes, in general, the way school is taught is where my disability is.
JERRY: Okay, so press on.
LESLEY: Press on! Hello! Did you hear what I just said? *(She said with a shocked look on her face.)* It is not so simple, Jerry.
JERRY: Come now, Lesley, this is just a small part of you. You are a remarkable woman who, I might add, has so much more going for you. Rise above it.
LESLEY: Look, I just found out and I'm a little upset, so give me a break.
JERRY: The world is nothing like college, Lesley.
LESLEY: Don't I know it!
JERRY: Once you're done with school, none of this will matter.
LESLEY: I'm not there yet, and this is tough.
JERRY: I know, but you can do it.
LESLEY: Those are big words.
JERRY: Words I know you can follow through on.
LESLEY: Yeah, so everybody tells me.

JERRY: So have you heard anything else from the IRS?

LESLEY: The IRS. That's right, thanks for reminding me. When I called and asked the individual about the $640.00 fee from taxes in 1991, the woman told me it was a renter's fee charged against me from John in Texas. I tried to explain to her that there was no written agreement between John and me and continued by telling her John and I had agreed I could stay there because he was living with his fiancée at the time. The woman told me I had to prove my innocence. Then I asked her how I was supposed to do such a thing when there was no written agreement between the two of us. She told me that was too bad, and if I could not prove my innocence, I would have to pay the money.

JERRY: What did you decide to do?

LESLEY: I called the sister of a true friend of mine who also lived in Texas. We became good friends there, even though we never really talked when she lived with her parents in Wausau. She knew about my situation with John, so I asked her to write me a certified letter that explained her side of the situation from the conversations we had about him.

JERRY: What if the letter doesn't work?

LESLEY: There is a student law service for general information and help. I'm going to go and see what kind of information I can obtain on this tax issue.

JERRY: Sounds like you're on the right track. Now why don't we go get something to eat?

LESLEY: Thanks, but I'm not really hungry.

JERRY: Been too rough of a day, huh?

LESLEY: Kind of more than I feel I can handle, actually.

JERRY: You can do it. Just hang in there, girl. Everything will work out.

LESLEY: I hope so. I just have to keep a positive attitude and remind myself to press on.

JERRY: I know you can do it.

LESLEY: Yeah, it just feels pretty heavy right now.

End of scene
4th Talent (my dance piece)

Act 2 Scene 3

This scene begins in Mary's office. Both are sitting.

MARY: What is it you came to see me for?

LESLEY, *looking at the audience*: Do you think these people ever talk to each other? *(Looks at Mary.)* I came here to set up a program to help me with my weakness. Didn't you get the results from the psychologist's office?

MARY: Yes, I did. What kind of assistance do you think you need?

LESLEY: I thought you would have some idea of what would help me.

MARY: No, this would be something you have to figure out, Lesley. I'm the person who puts your VISA together, you're the person who tells me what you think you need to help you get through school easier.

LESLEY: What I need is to be free from taking tests. That would help me a lot. What's a VISA?

MARY: It is a document with a list of your needs on it.

LESLEY: What do I need it for?

MARY: It will inform your teachers of the weakness you have.

LESLEY: You mean I have to tell the teachers?

MARY: It is advisable to do so.

LESLEY: Easy for you to say. Could I be free from taking tests?

MARY: Unfortunately, I cannot authorize that, Lesley, for that is the way of college. How else can your performance be tested if not by tests?

LESLEY: I don't know, I just don't feel a test is the proper way to judge someone's ability. I mean just because a person may do well on a test doesn't mean he or she will be able to apply it in life. How could being a good test taker make you good at surviving? Life is more difficult than a test on a piece of paper. What applies to one situation doesn't always apply to another.

MARY: This may be very true, Lesley, but it's always been this way and there are ways to overcome it, and that is what I am going to try and help you with.

LESLEY: You make it sound so easy.

MARY: It depends on you. Now let's try to find ways to help you in school. One of the things we can offer you is a notetaker and also longer time on the tests.

LESLEY: A notetaker would be great, but I'm not sure if I really need extra time on tests. (*Pause for a second*) Though it would be cool to have the services too.

MARY: We can authorize for you to take the test in another room. But there are some things you must do.

LESLEY: Oh, like what?

MARY: It is advisable for you to talk to the professors before classes start to let them know about your needs. Usually, they are willing to meet the needs of the student, but there are occasions when the professors don't feel they should have to do anything. Though this is rare, and the VISA I am preparing for you will HELP you in those situations.

LESLEY: Great. This way, the professor can make his or her judgment on me before the class even begins. I am not looking forward to this.

MARY: Also, with the notetaker, you can either ask a student in class or ask us, and we will hire one for you. Once you have a notetaker, you should arrange a time to meet him or her and give the individual the note-taking supplies he or she will need. It is also helpful to give the notetaker feedback on the notes. There is a form you need to fill out for the notetaker. And also an evaluation form on the performance of the notetaker. Which is to be given to us at the end of each semester.

LESLEY: I have to evaluate the notetaker?

MARY: Yes. There is another faculty member that will help you with the paperwork needed for the service. Her name is Julie, and I'll call her now to set an appointment (*Pause.*) Her name is Lesley (*Pause.*) Today at three. (*Looks up at Lesley who nods.*) That would be fine. (*Hangs up the phone and looks at Lesley.*) It's almost time for you to meet her, so we should set up another appointment to see me after you talk to her, and we will finish putting your VISA together.

LESLEY: Right after I see her?

MARY: Yes, it should only take you half an hour with her, and this will give me time to get the paperwork needed for your VISA.

LESLEY: Okay, I'll see you at three-thirty. (*They both get up, Lesley leaves.*)

Lesley walks past the receptionist's desk where Julie is waiting for her, and the two of them go into Julie's office.

JULIE: Please sit down.

LESLEY: Thank you.

JULIE: Now what is it I can help you with?

LESLEY, *looking out at the audience and shaking her head in disbelief*: I'm here to get the information needed for a notetaker.

JULIE: I have some paperwork you need to fill out in order to give you this service. Are you a Division of Vocational Rehabilitation client?

LESLEY: DVR client, yes, I am.

JULIE: Sometimes this service can be authorized by your DVR counselor. But if it is not, then we will cover the cost for you.

LESLEY: I will call my counselor and ask if they will pay for the service. But if not, then the program would cover the cost offered here? (*She says to make sure she understands.*)

JULIE: Yes, it will. Here is the paperwork needed for the service. All you need to do is fill it out and give it back to us as soon as possible. It is advisable for you to get a student in the class to take your notes for you because it is the most convenient. However, there is a risk when you do this because we cannot control his or her attendance. This is especially true during exam time. This is usually the time a student will skip a class to prepare for an exam. One of the things you can do is talk to the teacher before class begins and ask him or her to ask the class as a whole if anyone would take notes for you.

LESLEY, *with a surprised look*: In front of the whole class?

JULIE: Yes. (*With a concerned look.*) It's not that uncommon to have a notetaker, Lesley. You should try not to worry about it.

LESLEY: Don't worry about it. You tell me to have the professor announce to the whole class that I am unable to take my own notes? (*Pause.*) Do you realize what you have just said to me?

JULIE: There are many people who have a notetaker at this university, and they are doing just fine with it. You will find this resource to be a very beneficial one really, so try not to worry so much about it.

LESLEY: All I have to do. I can't believe you are saying this to me. When am I supposed to find time to do all of this?

JULIE: I know it seems difficult right now. but once you find ways to overcome your weakness, it won't be a weakness anymore.

LESLEY: Once I find ways to overcome my weakness, my weakness, this is going to take time, time of which I do not have much of, and you are telling me all I have to do. When am I supposed to find the time to do all this?

JULIE: That's something you have to figure out, Lesley. Now here is all the paperwork you need to fill out for this service. Double-ply paper will be supplied to the notetaker. This way you will get a copy of the notes at the end of class.

LESLEY: At least there is one less thing I have to do.

JULIE: Now remember to fill out the forms I have given you and bring it back to me as soon as you can. Also find out if DVR will help with this.

LESLEY: Okay, thank you for your time. (*As Lesley leaves the office, a young man she met in her physical education course greets her. They stop for a moment and talk.*)

BOY: How is it going?

LESLEY: Okay, considering.

BOY: Considering what?

LESLEY: Considering I just found out I have a learning disability as well as an anxiety problem.

BOY: Oh, really, a lot of information to digest. (*He says with a sincere look.*)

LESLEY: Yes, and all I keep hearing from these people is "all you have to do." And by the way, all I have to do is: find a notetaker, fill out forms for a notetaker, evaluate notetaker, put notes into visuals, find out what services I need to help compensate for my weakness, tell the professors about my weakness, and find/learn ways to overcome my anxiety problem. This, by the way, is outside of what the average student has to do. It has nothing to do with issues outside of school either. Which reminds me, I need to go to the Student Law Service to find any kind of information I can on the IRS issue. (*Heavy sigh.*) Jeez, I really don't think these people realize what they are saying to me. (*Looks up at boy.*) I bet you're glad you stopped and asked me how I was doing.

Boy, *looking at her and smiling:* Looks like you have your work cut out for you. You're having problems with the IRS. That must suck!

Lesley: Oh yes, and I might add, it has been a very painful one too. But I shouldn't bother you with that.

Boy: Good luck.

Lesley: Thank you.

Boy: For what?

Lesley: Listening.

They both smile and walk away from each other.

End of scene
5th talent.

Act 2 Scene 4

Jerry and Lesley are in the bar with drinks in hand. There are a few extras and the bartender.

Lesley: A toast to a good friend!

Jerry: Are you talking about me? (*He says jokingly.*)

Lesley: No, I'm talking to the bartender. (*She looks at him.*) Duh.

Jerry: Thank you. Why are you in such good spirits?

Lesley: I received a letter from the IRS today.

Jerry: And?

LESLEY: Basically, it said that because of new evidence, I didn't owe any money, and if I already started paying, I would receive the amount back.

JERRY: Good for you, Lesley.

LESLEY: Really, one less thing to worry about.

JERRY: What happened to John?

LESLEY: I decided not to concern myself with what happened to him. For my intention was not to hurt anyone. It was to win through honesty and persistence.

JERRY: Well, it worked.

LESLEY: As it should have, for honesty always pays off.

JERRY: How are things with school?

LESLEY: How are things with school? You know, Jerry, I really don't think those people understand what they are saying when they say "all you have to do."

JERRY: They probably don't, but this won't stop you, will it?

LESLEY: I've come too far to stop now, Jerry. It just feels so empty and alone from where I sit. I'm the one who is continuously reminded of my imperfections. I don't know whether to be envious or happy for those who don't have to struggle. On the one hand, to have your life given to you in a way where lessons are few yet fun is plenty, there would appear to be little worth in their life. Yet for those who struggle, there is not only a better understanding of the world and the people in it, but there is also a pain from the knowledge obtained from it.

The End

Life after Surgery

IT WAS JUST BEFORE Christmas in 1992 when Lesley found out she was not eligible for long-term disability. It was early in the morning when she received the call from work, notifying her that her short-term disability would run out by the end of the month. And it continued by stating she would not be eligible for long-term disability.

"*What!*" Lesley could not believe it. She asked the financial representative why and was told she did not wait long enough after she had her last epidural steroid shot to have surgery. Therefore, it was considered preexisting. Lesley's heart began to beat faster, and her body began to quiver as she listened to this person tell her destiny. She had no idea this was going to happen to her. She tried to explain to the individual that the insurance representative for the corporation told her she only had to wait six months after her last epidural shot to be eligible for long-term disability. The financial representative was empathetic and stated to be eligible for long-term disability, one would have to wait a year before it would no longer be considered preexisting. Since Lesley had back surgery nine months after her last epidural shot, nothing could be done. Lesley hung up the phone and sat there on her bed for a moment, trying not to believe what had just happened. She pinched herself to make sure she was awake. She was.

She felt as if she wanted to cry but couldn't. Her body just sat there on the edge of the bed in a state of confusion.

She started to pace the floors, trying to figure out what she was supposed to do. *My god*, she thought. *What on earth am I supposed to do? Where am I going to live? What am I to do about money?*

As she put her hand on her forehead, she grumbled:

"Ugh, and then there is school. What about school? I just started going to college. It's even paid for through a rehabilitation center. I don't want this situation to prevent my opportunity to go to college. Oh my god! *What am I supposed to do?*"

She took a deep breath and let out a heavy sigh. She decided to pick up the phone and call her friend. Barb was unable to talk with Lesley right away, so they decided to meet at the local bar at 6:00 p.m. When they met at the Moonlight, Lesley explained her situation to Barb, and before long, Barb told Lesley she could stay with her in her spare bedroom. Lesley was grateful and gave her a hug.

Initially, everything was fine. The two of them would talk about the past, sharing little secrets from earlier years that meant nothing now that they were older. One being a listener for the other and sharing laughs along the way. It even got to the point where the two of them thought about being roommates. Though Barb seemed a little more anxious about it than Lesley. Lesley felt they needed more time to see if they could be roommates.

One night while the two of them were at their local bar they met a woman. She stood about 5'5", looked to be about twenty-five, and weighed about one hundred twenty pounds. She had short dishwater blond hair with crystal blue eyes that were seated on a soft round face. Both Lesley and Barb were attracted to her immediately. After a few minutes, Lesley found out her name was Sunny, and she enjoyed being active. Lesley asked what type of sports Sunny enjoyed and realized they both liked bicycling. After talking for about five minutes, the two of them decided to meet each other the next day to talk some more about bicycling. As they were finishing the conversation about bikes, Barb joined in the conversation. It wasn't long before Barb took over the conversation. The three of them talked for a while and decided to meet again at the bar the following week, and Lesley kept her date with Sunny the next day.

It was 10:00 a.m. when Sunny met with Lesley at the park. They rode their bicycles through the park to an open area that was in the middle of the park. There were picnic benches and grills throughout the area. Sunny took out a blanket from the backpack she was carrying and set it on the grass. The two lay on the blanket to relax for a while. They were the only two in the area, and the sound of the breeze blew gently across their bodies as they lay there for a moment in silence.

Suddenly, Sunny leaned over and kissed Lesley. Lesley was taken by surprise yet responded to the tenderness of Sunny's touch. When their visit came to an end the two of them decided to see each other again to continue the relationship. They said their goodbyes, and Lesley went back to Barb's to talk about her day. A week had passed, and the evening came when Lesley and Barb were to meet Sunny at the bar. When they arrived at the bar, Barb told Lesley that Sunny was fair game even though Lesley was starting to date her. Lesley felt very hurt by this and totally disagreed with Barb's intentions. Barb eventually gained Sunny's attention, and Lesley was left with an uncomfortable feeling about the whole thing.

Two nights later, Barb met another woman in the bar. Her name was Marsha. Barb decided to take her home and introduce her to Lesley. Lesley and Marsha became very comfortable with one another, and by the end of the evening, Lesley had inadvertently gained Marsha's attention. After Marsha left, Barb began to talk about how attracted to Marsha she was. Lesley asked Barb what she was going to do about Sunny, and Barb laughed and said she wanted both of them.

The next night while Barb was sleeping and Lesley was doing her homework, Marsha called. Lesley answered the phone and told her that Barb was asleep but would leave a message. Marsha said she was glad Barb was asleep because she didn't call to talk to her. Lesley was taken by surprise and smiled when she heard this. The two talked for a while and then set up a date to see each other on Friday. The next day Lesley let Barb know about the date she made with Marsha.

Barb told Lesley it was no big deal and hoped she would enjoy herself with Marsha. Lesley was relieved and felt it was only fair since Barb was dating a woman Lesley was interested in. She could remember what Barb said when they had a talk about Sunny. She said it wasn't her fault Sunny liked her and not Lesley. And then Barb told Lesley to get over it and laughed. Lesley decided not to feel bad about her decision to date Marsha.

On the night of the date, Barb asked Lesley for the keys to the apartment. Lesley asked why, and Barb told her she could not handle the fact that Marsha wanted to see Lesley instead of her. Lesley found the situation revolting and asked Barb why it was okay for her to make advancements on someone she was interested in, and it was okay; yet it wasn't okay for her to do the same. Barb told her that was different because Sunny was attracted to her. Lesley tried to explain that the same thing happened to herself and Marsha. But Barb didn't hear a word Lesley said and just stood there with her hand open and asked for the key and told Lesley she had three days to find another place to live. Lesley asked her how she was supposed to get in when she got home that night, and Barb told her to knock on the door and she would open it.

Lesley found another place to stay and moved out of Barb's house three weeks after she had moved in. This time it was with an older man. It was her counselor's uncle, Bob. When Lesley talked to Arnoldo, she found out about his widowed uncle. Apparently, he lived in a house alone and had a couple of extra rooms that were empty. Arnoldo set up an appointment for the three of them to get together and talk about living arrangements. He also prepared her before they went to the house by letting her know how messy his uncle's house would be. When they got there, the house was a mess. There were boxes and magazines scattered everywhere. It looked like the place had not been cleaned in a year. There was a path going through all the rooms except for the living room, which was the cleanest room in the house. It was messy too; only there was a little more space to move around in. The three of them sat down and discussed the possibility of her moving into the house for free, and in return, she would clean the house and then keep it clean. After they agreed, she moved in.

Lesley was given a big room for her sleeping quarters and had to clean the room before she could put her furniture in it. The room was just a bit bigger than an efficiency apartment. She was able to put all her furniture in the room and had space to spare for her to stretch. Initially, Bob and Lesley got along well. Bob was very excited about getting his house cleaned, and Lesley was grateful she had a place to live. It took her some time cleaning, for the house was truly a disaster area. After a couple of weeks, she was able to make the house look presentable for people to visit.

It seemed as if she had just finished with cleaning the house when Bob asked Lesley to sit down to talk for a minute. She had an idea about what he wanted to talk about when he asked her to sit down. As he started to talk, she could tell he was going to ask her to leave. He felt he could not afford for her to be there and he apologized. Lesley said she understood and asked him how long she had before he wanted her out. He told her as soon as possible. She got up and went to her room.

After Lesley closed the door, she went and sat on her bed and cried. She felt drained. She could not believe this was happening to her. Not only did she have to find another place to stay, but she also had homework to do. She felt this man took advantage of her. It seemed ironic that he asked her to leave almost immediately after she finished cleaning his house. Once again, her heart felt heavy from the weight she was carrying. She thought about what this was going to entail. Having to find a place to live again. And the lifting; she was not supposed to lift anything above twenty pounds. Yet what was she supposed to do? Who could she call for help? Who *would* help her? Where was she supposed to live? How much more must she endure? She sat on her bed and sighed.

After a few moments, she remembered a conversation she had with a fellow worker from Dee Howard Company. Simultaneously, she picked up the phone, took a deep breath, and told herself to relax. She dialed the number and waited for someone to answer on the other end. It rang and rang until she was ready to hang up, and just as she was ready to put the receiver down, Dick picked up the phone. Lesley started to talk to Dick about her situation and asked him if he remembered the conversation they had before she had back surgery. He told her he did and continued by telling her that he was hardly ever at his house because he was staying with his fiancée most of the time. He continued by telling her he was just getting ready to leave when the phone rang. He also told her wanted someone out there since he was never home and he did not like the house being empty. He said the only time he went out there was to work on his part-time job as a tax consultant.

Lesley told Dick she really appreciated his help and would pick up the key the next day. Before they hung up, he told her which room would be hers and she needed to clean out the room before she moved into it. It had been the room he kept his dog in when he was younger, and now that he kept her outside, the room was empty. He told Lesley the room stunk of urine, and the mattress was torn up from the dog chewing on it. Dick told her she could throw the mattress out and put the box spring upstairs in the attic. He also told her where some strong cleaner was for her to use in the room to help get rid of the odor. They decided she would clean the room immediately and move in over the weekend. Lesley thanked him and hung up the phone. She sat there for a moment and then thought about her new residence and the chore she had to do before she moved in. Dog urine, yuck!

Lesley left in the morning to go pick up the key to her new residence. Dick gave her a key and directions to his house. Lesley hugged him and then went to the house to clean the bedroom. The drive out to his house seemed to take forever. He lived out in the country and down in the hollow. It took a half hour to get to Dick's house from where he worked.

When she got there, she looked at the land the house was on. the house was put on a small hill that led to the river. The house in itself was very old and was already put together before it was put on his land. The house used to be located right in the middle of San Antonio and was going to be torn down and replaced with new buildings. When Dick heard about this, he went to look at the house, decided he wanted it, and bought it. He had to have it cut in half and towed out to his property where he pieced it back together. The back end of the house was on a slope, so Dick put stilts on the two corners and a couple in the middle to give the house the support it needed. He then made a strong foundation to support the house.

The front of the house was on solid ground while brick held up the back of the house. In the back underneath the house is where the washer and dryer were. He also had the riding lawn mower, lots of wood, and a fenced-in area for hazardous materials. The house was old and looked old. Lesley decided to go inside the house. She opened the front door and stepped in. She looked to her right and there was the living room. It was big and octagon in shape.

Lesley noticed an antique cannon in the room and wondered why someone would want to keep something like that inside. She turned her head forward and looked down the long corridor that led to the back porch. *Wow,* she thought, *that's far.* She looked to her immediate left, and there was the door to Dick's office. It was locked. She looked at the door next to the office door and opened it. She couldn't believe what she saw.

The room was full of junk. There was a table in the center of the room that had cement bags on top of it. There was wood scattered everywhere. Behind the door was a big bag of nails, screws, and mis-cellaneous junk. Against the wall on the far right of the room were beehive boxes. The room also had a refrigerator and antique cabinet in it. She left the room and felt grateful she didn't have to clean it. She started walking down the corridor and right before the opening to the kitchen was a gun rack on the right. Dick was a collector of guns from antique to brand-new. It was locked also. Lesley walked through the opening and entered the kitchen. The kitchen table was on the right almost immediately as she walked through the door. She turned to the left and walked through another opening that went into the other part of the kitchen.

Immediately to the right, as she walked through the opening was the stove and on the other side of the stove was a countertop that curved to the left until it met the sink. On the other side of the sink was more countertop, and then the refrigerator was in the corner. She looked left of the refrigerator and noticed a window that looked out into the woods. Next to the window was a cabinet filled with canned goods. On the left side of the room was a wall with a closed-in pantry at the center. She set her hand on the breakfast bar which was right behind the stove and noticed the phone and answering machine was on the other end of the bar.

Lesley stepped out of the kitchen and walked to the room just beyond the breakfast bar on the left. She opened the door and shut it quickly. This was going to be her room. She could not believe the odor in the room. *My god,* she thought. *I'm supposed to clean this room, ugh.* She needed to step away for a moment to get a breath of fresh air. She decided to go look at the back porch, which took two steps to get to. The porch was closed in and viewed the backyard. She looked at how large the backyard was and remembered Dick telling her there was a river behind his house. There were trees that blocked the view of the river, so she decided to go and take a look at it. She felt she needed to mentally prepare herself for the chore she had to do.

March was in the air, and though it was a warm night, the breeze felt good. Lesley walked to the wooded area behind the house and found the river. She found a tree she could sit on while she watched the river flow downstream. She thought of how peaceful it was out there in the boonies and decided to go back up to the house and clean her room.

From school, Dick's house was about an hour away. Which meant two hours a day would be spent on driving alone, and Lesley didn't really like that. She felt she was wasting so much time on just driving alone. If she wanted to go out after she got home from school, it meant different things too. She would not only be driving home late when it was dark and the roads were secluded, but she would also be greeted by an old empty house out in the middle of nowhere. And then there were the sounds of the house. At night, she would lay in bed and try to keep herself calm as the house moaned and groaned.

Lesley did not feel very comfortable out there in the boonies, all by herself in Dick's big house that cried throughout the night. Sounds like footsteps or the howling of the wind as it blew through the vents up in the attic. It took her a week to get used to the sounds of the house, and though she knew where the noises were coming from, it did not give her the comfortable feeling she wanted. She would think about how no one would know if something happened to her out there. There were a couple of neighbors, but both lived on top of the hill. One of them was on top of the hill where Lesley would turn left to get to Dick's house at the bottom of the hill. The other one was right across the street from the house only on top of the hill.

A week after she moved into her new residence, she received a phone call from Dick. His fiancée told him he had to inform her about his ex-girlfriend who was a little psychotic. *Great!* thought Lesley, *Like I need some psycho from Dick's past bothering me.* She hung up the phone and thought of how nice it was of Dick to wait until she was moved into the house to tell her this information. Lesley stood by the phone and sighed. She had just moved out there, and already there was a problem. She was beginning to wonder when this roller-coaster ride she was on would stop and let her exhale. She felt as if she had no control over her life and like a puppet left hanging on to life by a thread.

Since it was the beginning of the year, Dick was at the house more than he usually was because he was doing taxes for people. Lesley didn't mind this because then she wasn't alone in the house. One night while Lesley was sitting on her bed reading her notes, the phone rang.

Since Dick was home, Lesley decided to let him answer it. After it rang a couple of times, he picked it up in his office. The conversation was short, and Lesley heard him slam the phone down just minutes after he picked it up. He got up and went to Lesley's room to tell her to let the answering machine pick up if the phone rang again. Seconds after he went back into his office, the phone rang and rang until the answering machine picked up. Since Lesley's room was right by the kitchen and the phone and answering machine was right outside her room, she heard the whole message. A woman by the name of Tracey was on the other line, and she decided to leave a message for Dick.

"I know what you did to my son. He told me about it. I want you to call me so we can talk about it! I know you are there! Pick up the phone, or I will press charges." There was a pause and Tracey continued. "Look, I will not press charges if you take me back." When she realized Dick was not going to pick up, she changed her tone again.

"Dick! I am going to tell the police you molested my son. If you do not pick up, I am going to do it! If you take me back, I won't."

This went on for over a minute and finally, she hung up. Lesley lay on her bed and wondered about the accusations this woman was throwing at Dick. Dick was letting her stay there for free, and he didn't seem the type. She thought about Dick for a minute and then the message and decided she wouldn't believe the woman. She also felt a conversation with Dick on the subject would make her feel better.

When she talked to Dick about the crazy woman, he told Lesley it was a mistake for him to ever date this Tracey girl, but he felt sorry for her. He knew she had a son that was being neglected, so he gave her money to get the boy some nice things and he also spent time with him. Since the boy didn't have a father, Dick was trying to fill the gap. He also said he knew she was a little twisted but didn't think she would act in the way she did. He said the reason he went out with her was because he felt sorry for the kid. She drank a lot and never really took care of her son properly, so he would do things for him. He looked at Lesley and said he wished he had never dated Tracey. Lesley looked at him and asked how his fiancée felt about what was happening with the psycho woman. He told Lesley it was not helping his relationship at all. Julie was getting nervous about the calls she was receiving at work. This was Tracey's way of trying to hurt Dick, and it was beginning to take its toll on his relationship.

One Saturday afternoon, Lesley decided she was going to go out for a while and enjoy some company. She took a bath in the bear claw bathtub and got ready to go out. Lesley enjoyed the bathtub. It was a big deep bathtub that covered her whole body from the neck down to her toes. She always felt relaxed after she got out of the bathtub. Though it would only last for a short while because she always felt a little uncomfortable in that house, especially at night. She looked at her watch and noticed it was almost 6:00 p.m. She thought she better get going since it was going to take her forty-five minutes to get there. She decided food would be the first stop, and then she would go to the local bar.

There was a soft breeze on this May evening, and Lesley arrived at the bar at approximately 8:00 p.m. As she entered the bar, Lesley noticed a couple of women playing a game of pool on the right. She smiled at them and walked on toward the bar. When she reached the bar, she ordered a drink. The bartender gave her a drink and said it was taken care of. Lesley thanked the bartender and asked who it was from. The bartender pointed to a woman across the bar from them and said, "She told me she owed you a drink."

Lesley looked at the woman and noticed it was Marsha. She smiled and thanked her by nodding her head. Marsha smiled and gestured for Lesley to join her. Lesley went to join Marsha for a couple of drinks. The two of them talked about the place Lesley was living in. Lesley told Marsha how difficult it was to get used to the noises in the house, especially at night. She told Marsha it usually took her an hour to fall asleep because of the noises in the old house. Especially in the attic which was only one flight above her. Sometimes it would sound like someone was trying to get in through the window or even someone walking across the floor. And the stairs that led to the attic were right off the kitchen, by the table, just a couple of feet from her bedroom door. She paused for a moment and then she looked at Marsha and told her how beautiful the land was. She talked about the river and the tree branch that she sat on when she wanted to relax.

Marsha told Lesley that the scenery sounded nice, but the house sounded like it would take some getting used to. Lesley smiled and looked at her watch. It was almost midnight, and she had a long ride home, so she decided to leave. She said her goodbyes and left.

Dick's dog, Eva, greeted her at the front gate with enthusiasm. It was just before 1:00 a.m. when she arrived home, and the outside light was burnt out which made it a little spookier around the house. It was dark out, so she was glad that Eva was there. After Lesley walked through the gate, she had to tell the dog to get down. She walked to the house while Eva jumped all around her along the way. She unlocked the door, told Eva to get down, and went inside. Once she was inside, she got ready for bed. Lesley had just laid her head on the pillow when the phone rang. She got out of bed and answered the phone. It was the operator with a collect call from Tracey. Lesley told the operator she would not accept the collect call and said Dick wasn't there. Lesley went back to bed and tried to fall asleep. It was 1:50 a.m. and suddenly, the phone rang again. Lesley was just starting to fall asleep, and she did not appreciate the phone ringing. It rang four times before Lesley picked up. It was another collect call from Tracey, though this time she used a pseudo name. Lesley told the operator Dick was not there and hung up the phone. She went back to bed and tried to go back to sleep.

Bang! *Yelp*! Lesley lifted the covers and started walking down the corridor to the front door. As she walked past the kitchen table and down the long hallway to the door, she opened the door, and the person on the other side was Tracey.

This was the first time Lesley saw Tracey. She was short with black hair and brown eyes. The woman stood there and blurted out: "I just want you to know I have a gun and shot the dog!" Lesley looked at Tracey with a look of questionable surprise.

"What are you doing here?"

"I want to talk to Dick."

"I told you Dick is not here. I told you this when you called."

"Look, lady, he has done some things to my son."

"I don't want to hear it. I have my own things to deal with!"

"Can I use your phone?"

"You tell me you have a gun and you shot the dog, and now you want to use the phone. I don't think so."

"Could you call Dick?"

"I do not know his number."

Screeeeech! The car that gave Tracey a ride took off.

"Oh my god, now what!"

Tracey looked in the direction of the noise and then back at Lesley.

"I want to talk to Jack! Do you even care what is going on with my child and Dick?"

"I have enough problems of my own, and I do not need to get involved with your particular problem. I have never met you in my life, and you have a gun and shot the dog. This is between you and Dick, and I cannot help you there. Please leave!"

Tracey started to leave then turned around and turned back and up the porch.

"Don't you care about what Dick is doing to my son?"

"What I know is you have a gun and you shot the dog! Please leave!"

Tracey finally left, and Lesley shut the door as Tracey shut the gate. As Lesley started walking down the corridor to her room, she thought about how invaded she felt. *Bang*! Another gunshot. Lesley shuddered and went to the phone to dial 911. As she got closer to the phone, she realized she needed the address of where she lived and remembered how no one she has talked to has ever heard of the address where she lives. She thought to herself, *Address, address—oh my god, what if the police do not know where this house is?* She looked at the cupboard, and there was nothing with the address on it. "Shit, I need to find mail with the address on it!" She turned around to the kitchen table, and there she found a bill with the address on it.

"Whew, thank God." A heavy sigh followed. She turned back to the countertop where the phone was and dialed 911.

Lesley knelt down next to the breakfast bar and wrapped her arms around her knees. "This is 911, what is your emergency?"

"My name is Lesley, and a woman with a gun came to my house and shot the dog."

"Calm down, ma'am, I will send a police officer out there right away, but first I need the address."

"The address is: 1234 Oak Street. Oh my, are the police going to know where this place is?"

"Yes, the officer who took the call knows where you are. Are you alone?"

"Yes, I am alone, and Eva, the dog, was shot!"

"Ma'am, I understand. Just be patient and the police will be there soon."

"Okay, bye."

"Bye."

Lesley then called Dick and told him what happened.

"Dick, Tracey shot the dog and she needs to go to the veterinarian."

"Lesley, there is a shotgun behind the door on the back porch. It is loaded. If she comes back, use it. There is a twenty-four-hour clinic by the airport. I will meet you and Eva there."

"Okay, but first I have to wait for the police to get here, and after we are done, I will call you before I leave."

Two police cars pulled down in front of Dick's house. Lesley went to the front door and opened it. She stepped outside where the officers could see her.

"Ma'am, do you know the windows are shot out of your car?'

"Great! Now I need windows for my car." Lesley told the police what happened and asked if they could go under the house in the back to make sure the crazy lady wasn't there. She wasn't. They walked back to the front of the house and discussed where she might have gone. Suddenly, van lights on top of the hill turned on. One of the officers left the area to check out where the vehicle was going and who was in it while the other stayed with Lesley. The two of them continued talking about what happened, when suddenly, another call came in from his partner asking for backup. He left and Lesley was standing there alone, and the realization of not knowing where the dog was encompassed her body. She started to walk toward the back of the house, calling Eva's name as she walked. There was no answer.

She looked at the door behind the house where the washer and dryer were. She thought about going in, but her nerves wouldn't let her. She decided to call 911 again and asked the operator if she would ask one of the officers who responded to the call earlier where the dog was.

"This is the woman who called earlier about the dog being shot by the crazy woman, and I was wondering, could you ask one of the officers who came out here if they know where the dog is?"

"Ma'am, you need to stay there until one of the officers comes to get a statement."

"I need to get the dog to the vet because she has been shot."

"Ma'am, I understand. An officer will be there in a minute to take your statement, and then you can take the dog to the vet," the operator said with empathy in her voice.

"Fine, I will wait. Please tell them to hurry though. Goodbye."

The officer arrived within five minutes. The two sat down, and Lesley gave the officer her statement. After this was done, the two of them went outside to look for the dog. The two of them found Eva under the house by the fence in shock. Lesley had to go behind her and lift up her legs to help her along the way. Once Lesley got Eva to move a little, the officer gave her a rope to tie loosely around Eva's neck so they could get her out from under the house and into Lesley's car. The officer reminded Lesley that her car seats were full of glass and needed to be cleaned before Eva could be put in it. Lesley went and got a couple of her towels, wiped the glass off the seats, and put the towels on the seat to prevent Eva's blood from staining her car. Then she took Eva and helped her into the car. When she finished, she thanked the police officer and went into the house to call Dick and let him know she was on her to the vet. Dick said he would meet her there.

Lesley got in her car and started driving to the vet off Broadway in San Antonio. She looked at Eva as they were driving and told her everything was going to be okay. Eva just sat patiently as Lesley drove down the highway. As they started getting closer to the city, Lesley was thinking about what she should do after she dropped off the dog. She definitely didn't want to go back to the house in the boonies. She felt safer on the dark roads than she did in that house. Oh, what was she to do? She thought for a moment and decided to call her friend Sharon. Sharon was a close friend of hers from her hometown in Wausau. Lesley looked at the dog and thought she looked okay and stopped in a shopping plaza to call her friend.

When Sharon picked up the phone, Lesley apologized for calling her at such an early hour and then explained her situation to her. When Lesley asked if she could stay with her overnight, Sharon told her she would have the front light on and to just ring the bell. Lesley told Sharon she had to drop the dog off and talk to Dick first. Sharon told her to just ring the bell, and someone would answer.

Lesley and Eva waited ten minutes before Dick and his fiancée showed up at the vet's. Lesley was slightly irritated with them since they only lived ten minutes from there. Eva was already in the doctor's office, waiting for Dick to get there to sign some paperwork. After Dick signed the paperwork, he talked to Lesley about her window's. He gave her a signed check to take care of the windows. Lesley thanked him and left. When Lesley got to Sharon's house, it was already becoming daylight. She gave Sharon a rundown of the evening then went to bed.

After Lesley fixed her windows, she found out Dick and his soon to be family were to move into the house. Dick told Lesley she had to clean the room next to the office because that was going to be her new room when they moved out there. Lesley told him she could not lift up the things that were in the room. He told her he would find someone, but he never did. Lesley had to find a couple of men to help her get the room cleaned. She didn't really know either one of the men that helped her.

She told them she would supply the beer if they would help her, and they did. After the room was cleaned, Lesley only spent a couple of nights in it. The reason: her car broke down.

It happened when she was going to her newly found friend Beetle. The clutch went out as soon as she turned down the street Beetle lived on. So Lesley drove it into her driveway and parked it. Beetle was a very messy person, and she knew it. She let Lesley know about it as soon as she walked in the door. It was very obvious to Lesley that Beetle's house was a mess. She blamed work for the reason it was not clean. They both knew better. Beetle then offered Lesley the use of her place while she was getting her car fixed. Lesley took her up on the offer and thanked her.

It was the middle of June when Lesley's car broke down, and Lesley wasn't able to fix it because she didn't have the money. She ended up staying at Beetle's house. Lesley felt she could not endure any more of what was going on in her life. It seemed no matter what she did, nothing but obstacles got in the way. She was tired of moving and wondered what all of it meant. She felt her only option was to go back to Wausau, Wisconsin, with her parents. She could no longer be a part of Texas. Though she loved it there, she needed to leave for her mind's sake. She told Beetle her decision and then she told Dick.

After Lesley made the decision to go back home, everything went smoothly. Sharon's husband used his credit card to rent a U-Haul. Shortly after she picked up the truck, she went to load it up. When she got to Dick's house, he and his new wife were there. Neither one of them offered to help her load Lesley's things into the truck. As Lesley was loading the truck, Dick asked Lesley if she went and filed a report against Tracey. She didn't. So, they took his sports car, the three of them, and yes, Lesley's legs were in her face.

What an asshole, she thought. First he watched her load a truck, and then he put her in a car made for two. After Lesley filed the complaint, she left for Wisconsin.

Lesley cried when she left San Antonio, Texas. She thought about the last six months of her life and wondered why all these things happened to her. She felt her kindness was taken advantage of in a big way. She felt as if she had lost, been defeated, or even conquered. Going back to Wausau hurt her insides. What would her family think? She wondered what kind of lesson she was supposed to learn from what happened. Was it a lesson given to her before, but she did not learn from it? Maybe it was given to her over and over, but she just didn't get it. *God,* she thought as she rolled her eyes.

Why did all this shit happen? What was the lesson? She decided she would pay more attention to the fine print of things and to choose her friends more carefully. She also realized bad things can and do happen to good people. The lesson would be to learn from it and try not to let it happen again.

This next story is an interview with my mother about her son (my brother), and some of the experiences she has had to endure with not only him but the doctors as well.

Riley-Day Syndrome

RILEY-DAY SYNDROME, OR FAMILIAL dysautonomia (FD), is a rare disease that usually affects Ashkenazi Jews. Riley, Day, and colleagues first described it in 1948. Characterized by both high and low blood pressure, cyclical vomiting, and feeding difficulties, difficulty in swallowing and aspiration, diminished or absent lacrimation (secretion of tears), diminished pain sensation, excessive sweating, and absence of the fungi-form papilla (little bumps) of the tongue. Along with this are mental retardation, emotional instability, skin blotching, and seizures (Pediatr 312).

My brother Keith was born on March 11, 1962, at the Wausau Hospital in Wausau, Wisconsin. It was around a month after Mom took him home when she had her first experience with his disability. I was only a year and a half at the time. It was on a weekend when Keith was feeling very warm to Mother. She took a thermometer and put it under his arm. The marker soared to the top of the thermometer, which is about 108 degrees. She called the doctor and calmly asked him what she should do. He found it hard to believe that his temperature could be so high and told her to give him a cool sponge bath, and if the temperature did not go down by the morning, to take him to the hospital. Mom stayed up all night long with Keith, sponging him down with cool water to help keep him cool, and with her gentle voice, she would talk to him.

The next morning, Mom took Keith to the hospital. His temperature was down from the long night before. So the doctor said he was okay and to go home. Mother did not like this answer and stated that Keith was not well, so they pacified her and kept him in the hospital overnight for observation.

The night came, and with it, Keith's temperature. The nurses were frantic when they experienced that evening with Keith. Never had they seen a person reach such a temperature before. It was only after the nurses called the doctor and stated the same thing my mother did the night before, before he believed it to be true.

He called Mom the next day to apologize for his disbelieving her earlier. He continued by saying he wanted Keith to go to The UW Madison Hospital for some testing. In the hospital, the staff did all kinds of kidney examinations. Keith was there for one month before they finished testing him. In the end, the doctors could only tell Mom what was not wrong with him and that his nerve endings were smaller than normal.

On the way home from Madison, Keith started getting warm, and Mom started getting worried. They stopped in Stevens Point Hospital to see about getting Keith's temperature taken. They would not help. Apparently, according to the hospital policy, he would have to be admitted before his temperature could be taken. Mom only wanted to see if she needed to ice him down, or if he would be okay until he got home. They ended up going to a clinic in Stevens Point, and the doctor there was very nice. He took Keith's temperature, and it was high. The doctor told Mom that Keith would be okay for the drive, and he did not charge for the visit. One month had gone by, and there was no knowledge of why Keith had such high temperatures, and they went home that night with worry on their mind, for there was no resolution from the hospital.

With time, Mom became more aware of Keith's condition. She learned to look for certain signs to alert her at the times when something was the matter with him. In the earlier years, Mom used to worry when Keith would laugh or cry real hard because he would hold his breath, and Mom would have to hold his tongue down and watch his eyes roll back while his body stiffened. Mom considered these seizures, but the doctors said he was only holding his breath.

Mom kept Keith in a crib longer than the rest of us. She felt it protected him better, and it probably did. He slept in a crib until he was around four or five. One night, she noticed that his right hip was swollen, so she took him to the hospital the next day. Keith was admitted to the hospital, and Mom received a phone call from the doctor the following day. He wanted to know what she did to Keith. He said it looked as if someone took him by the leg and swung him around. Mom could not believe the doctor was questioning her in such a way and insinuating it was done on purpose. She cried hysterically after that conversation.

In five weeks, Keith had nine operations on his hip, and throughout the whole excursion, he always kept positive. Mom called him her little charmer because he always knew how to smile. She really didn't like leaving him in the Madison Hospital and would cry every time she would leave. The hospital had beds lined up in the hallway. The nurses' station had paper scattered about and the hallways looked like a dungeon. When Mom went to visit Keith, she had to look at him through a little window because of the uncertainty of his illness. Mom's heart would break as she looked at Keith in that room by himself, looking at her, wanting to be held. Being so close yet so far. Wanting to touch, but not being allowed. The two would look at each other, and by some inward way, give strength to one another.

These things made it very difficult for Mom, but she knew Keith would be okay because the nursing staff there was wonderful.

When Keith went into the hospital for his hip, Mom and Dad did not have insurance. So the state paid for the medical costs. The only thing was the doctors would be picked for him. It just so happened Keith was given the best doctors on staff. Mom claimed it was because of the rarity of his illness. The doctor told Mom there were only thirteen cases in the United States and Europe in the 1960s.

She had a difficult time going upstairs while Keith was in the hospital for his hip. Every time she went upstairs, she would remember how the doctor accused her initially. She would put her children's clothes away and then sit on the top step and cry. While she sat there crying, she would wonder how Keith hurt himself and how to prevent it from happening again. When Keith came home from the hospital, the doctors did not feel he would ever be able to walk again. Before leaving the hospital, Mom asked the doctor what she should do if Keith tried to get up and walk. The doctor told Mom Keith would not be able to walk. She asked him again, and his reply was the same.

Finally, after going back and forth for a few minutes on this topic, the doctor said if Keith tried to walk, let him. But he went on by stating it will not happen. The first day Keith was home after this conversation, he pulled himself up by holding Mom's chair, wobbled a little, and then stood up. Shortly afterward, he was walking.

When Mom took him to the doctor for his checkup, the doctor was shocked. He could not believe Keith was walking. He asked if he could take Keith to a conference to show his colleagues this miraculous happening. He said it was the only way they would believe him. How could such a miracle happen? Inner strength, love—well, lots of love—and calcium buildup.

United Way nurses went to Keith twice a day for a long period of time to give him his shots to prevent infection in his hip. Keith went through quite a few nurses during the healing process of his hip. Mom told me they ranged from real assholes to extremely compassionate women. From one end of the spectrum, they looked everything over in the apartment, questioning the right my family had to own anything because of the free medical help Keith was given.

To the other end where the nurses would go out of their way to do nice things for Mom and Keith. You see, there were specific times the nurses would go to the house and administer the shot. Mom and Keith had to be there at this specific time. He would receive one in the morning and the other at five o'clock.

Mom told me about the first woman who cared for Keith.

She said it was this woman who truly showed her how to tend to Keith's wounds. She was like a sergeant. She went through the whole process with Mom. Telling her to wear plastic gloves whenever she cleaned Keith. She showed how to take the gloves off. Mom was learning how to be a nurse. Well, she had to learn.

The other woman Mom told me about was Mrs. Butler, and she was a widow. Mom said she was a wonderful woman. She recalled one Sunday night when Mrs. Butler gave Keith his shot at 7:30 p.m. instead of 5:00 p.m. so that the family could go out for a Sunday drive.

The nurses from United Way asked my mom to take Keith to a fundraiser to help raise money for the special children of society. Mom felt since the United Way helped her, she would take Keith to one of the events. She told me she would never do it again because of the ignorance in our society. Apparently, when she took him to one of the benefits held in a factory, the people would look at Keith and whisper to one another. She said she cried that day and decided she would never subject her son to such treatment again.

Initially, it was a struggle between Mom and the doctors when dealing with Keith, until the doctors decided to work with mom to help Keith in the best way possible. When this happened, things worked a little better. However, it was still difficult to deal with the many issues Keith seemed to be constantly battling with.

Keith was seven years old when Mom accomplished potty training him. It took Mom a month to do it. What she did was make sure to feed him the same breakfast, lunch, and supper every day and at the same time every day. Then she paid attention to when he went to the bathroom. She would give him a treat when he went to the bathroom on the toilet. If he went number one (pee), he would get one piece of candy, and if he went number two (poop), he was given two pieces. The whole family became a part of this. Whenever any of us went to the bathroom, we would tell Mom and made sure it was done in front of Keith. Eventually, he was potty trained.

It wasn't until Keith was seven or eight when the doctors said he had Riley traits. With the mental retardation, the doctors felt it was a part of the disease. Mom felt it was caused by the high fevers he had when he was a baby. She felt great sadness many nights when she could only look at Keith because holding him could only cause his temperature to rise. To love a child so much and not be able to help rid the pain—such sadness this is for a mother. To look upon her child and yearn with all the mightiest thoughts to cure her little baby from such unbearable things and still be unable to do a thing. Except for love, Mom had a lot of love for him.

Around the same time he was potty trained, he had problems with his knee. He had a hairline fracture and had to wear a brace for many years. I'm not sure when it was when Keith could not walk anymore. From what I understand, one day he took a few steps and then fell, got up, and tried again, but the same thing happened. I know it was before 1982, but I am not sure of the exact date.

While Keith was on the brace for his right leg, his big toe started to look like a prune. Then the skin just started ripping. The skin was shredded. Mom took him to the doctor, and he was admitted. Shortly after his admittance, his toe was amputated. Then from the added pressure put on the next two toes, the same thing happened again. So he now has two little toes on his right foot instead of five.

After I graduated high school in 1978, Keith's arm just swelled up. There were no signs whatsoever. While his arm was swollen, he had difficulty eating and what went down usually came back up. When she took him to the doctor, he was admitted immediately. Shortly afterward, he had surgery on his right elbow. When it was time to release Keith, the doctor wanted to speak to Mom before he left. When she went to see the doctor, the two sat down and talked. He started asking her questions about Keith to see if she would be able to take care of him. After being asked several questions, Mom found out the reason she was there, and it was because of how Keith looked when he went into the hospital. Since he was unable to eat properly because of the infection in his arm, he wasn't able to keep food down, and when he was admitted he looked a little thin. Because of this, he did not know whether or not Mom could handle Keith. Mom expressed how sick her son was and any one with such an infection would look poorly too. "He is my son and he is coming home with his mother!"

I joined the military in 1979, and while I was in, my brother was hospitalized twice for his arm. It seemed that no matter how well-nurtured his injury was, it would not get better. For three years, Keith and Mom dealt with his right arm.

I was stationed in Germany when I received a phone call from Mom. She told me Keith was in the hospital for his arm, and it didn't look good. I flew home after I made arrangements with the military to get a special leave of absence. When I got home, I went to the UW Madison Hospital with Dad. When we got there, the nurses were changing his gauge. I decided to wait outside because I couldn't stand the sight of blood. Dad decided to watch them change it, and he stood with his back to the door and faced Keith. I stepped outside the door and waited.

A minute went by, and I couldn't help but peek inside. The first time I did it, I couldn't see anything except for my dad. However, one time I looked, Dad had moved to the side, and I got to see Keith's hurt arm. The location was the right arm between the shoulder and elbow. The circumference of the wound was bigger than a baseball. I turned back quickly and took in a breath of air. After the doctor was done with the bandage, he came out and talked to Dad and I. The first words out of his mouth were that they were going to save his arm. What? I saw the arm and knew better. I asked the doctor if he had read Keith's records and continued by saying I'm sure you have. I listened to what he said and left. One week after I left to go back to Germany, they amputated his arm. When Keith left Madison, he was in diapers.

Keith has been home since the incident with his arm. Though he has had this disease throughout all of his life, he has never let it bring him or others down. He was an inspiration for me when I was a child, and he continues to be one for me now. He has taught many people patience, love, and genuine kindness. What seems to be a disability could be a blessing too.

As far as Mom, well, let's just say she is tired. Life has thrown her many challenges. Some of which hurt her deeply. Through it, she has become a very strong woman. I have a lot of respect for my mother. I asked her to give me a quote when dealing with Keith and his intellect. Her first response was, "He's got a memory like an elephant." Then she turned to me and said, "He is my little charmer."